90E

# CHILDREN AND DIVORCE

GARLAND REFERENCE LIBRARY
OF SOCIAL SCIENCE
(VOL. 119)

# CHILDREN AND DIVORCE
*An Annotated Bibliography and Guide*

Evelyn B. Hausslein

GARLAND PUBLISHING, INC. • NEW YORK & LONDON
1983

**Library of Congress Cataloging in Publication Data**

Hausslein, Evelyn B., 1938–
  Children and divorce.

  (Garland reference library of social science ; v. 119)
  Includes index.
  1. Children of divorced parents—Bibliography.
2. Children of divorced parents—Juvenile literature—
Bibliography.  I. Title.  II. Series.
Z5814.C5H28  1983  [HQ777.5]  016.3068′9  81–48420
ISBN 0–8240–9391–7

Printed on acid-free, 250-year-life paper
Manufactured in the United States of America

# CONTENTS

# INTRODUCTION

There is little need to cite statistics on the number of children who have experienced a divorce in their family. Anyone who works with children and their families is confronted with an increasing variety of family configurations. Such a person's ability to work effectively with an individual child may depend on the adult's level of comfort in accepting the style of family the child lives in and in working with that family. Although this bibliography is entitled *Children and Divorce*, a more accurate description might be "children living through marital transition." The upheaval caused by transition and change can occur when there is a separation in the family of origin or when the single parent or visiting parent changes into a two-parent family with its various step-relationships. The marital transition can go from a divorcing family, to a single parent and visiting parent or co-parenting relationship, to a possible stepfamily with its various relationships.

Wheelock College in Boston has offered a course for several years entitled "Children and Divorce." Participants in the course are primarily teachers, but others have been guidance counselors, social workers, a child therapist, and a few lawyers. One of the exciting aspects of the course is the interchange which takes place among people from various disciplines, and particularly the sharing of resources from different professional perspectives.

Most people who enroll are seeking information about the research in the area of children and divorce. The course provides this information; it also seeks to develop a more understanding attitude toward the problems and potential of children experiencing a divorce. A recurring theme is the importance of sharing information and insights with other professionals who are working with the family going through that experience. Those providing therapy for children need to talk with those, besides parents, who are on the front line: the teachers, child care workers, camp counselors, even babysitters. Teachers in turn need to feel comfortable knowing when and where to refer a child who seems to need more help than the individual teacher can offer in the classroom.

Adults contemplating a divorce or faced with an impending separation often turn for advice to a variety of professionals besides their friends. Some go first to a lawyer; others turn to the clergy. Some adults go to a physician whom they have trusted over a long period. They seek advice on staying together or separating, on how and what to tell the children, and on what types of custodial arrangements to set up. Therapists are turned to sometimes during the crisis and sometimes after initial arrangements have been made.

In the author's experience, there is not enough interchange among professionals from different disciplines or between those professionals working with children and those working with adults. This bibliography attempts to bridge this gap by bringing together articles and books from many different disciplines and suggesting the various professional and lay audiences for which they are relevant.

## Works Cited

This annotated bibliography of books, magazines, and journals will serve as a useful reference guide to research and service programs for those in the helping professions who work with children and families experiencing divorce. Books and articles written from 1975 through 1980 constitute a major portion of the bibliography. References from an earlier period that are seminal to an understanding of the field have been included either because of the contribution of the authors to our understanding of family life after divorce or because of the uniqueness of an idea which has not received attention recently in published literature. Availability to the public was also a criterion for inclusion in the bibliography. Each entry in the bibliography could be located in one or more libraries in the Boston area and is likely to be available in most major cities.

An attempt has been made to indicate which articles are based on research studies and which are written by practitioners who reflect their clinical experience. In some instances a few words have been said about sample size or age of population studied. No attempt has been made to discuss the study results since this would inevitably do an injustice to the complexity of the topic studied. The quality of research represented in the articles varies considerably. Some of the studies cited use small sample sizes or do not include comparison groups. Some authors acknowledge their efforts as pilot studies; others do not. Some articles report on completed studies that offer real insight into the issues concerning children and divorce. Other articles report on early findings of studies in process. One welcomes the increase in the last five years of research in this area. It is nonetheless important to acknowledge that much of our understanding is based on limited studies and all research should be read carefully to understand the validity of its results.

Those articles not based on research may offer a review of the literature or a discussion of successful clinical strategy. When relevant, the author's professional background or personal experience with divorce is indicated.

The language of the original or phrases from the abstract provided by the author have sometimes been used in the annotations.

## Organization

The major part of this book is a basic bibliographic list, alphabetized by author's name, which includes books and articles on child-centered or parenting issues directed to a professional audience. In addition to a brief annotation, each entry indicates the categories of professionals who may find the articles most useful.

The major list is supplemented by four other reference lists. The first includes books and articles to which professionals can refer parents. The second includes books that are appropriate for children and young adults. The third is a list of audio-visual materials on this topic. The fourth list contains names and addresses of organizations working with children and families or offering resource directories to families seeking guidance.

## Categorical Notations

A categorical notation system is used to indicate the usefulness and appropriateness of each book or article for different professional audiences: those working in a counseling role with children or with adults, and those working in a direct service, non-counseling role with children or with adults. An attempt has been made to introduce the interested professional to relevant articles from a wide variety of professional journals. There are four categories:

*Category 1*—Teachers and others who give direct service in a non-counseling role to children.

Entries with a category 1 designation are relevant, not to any particular job or role, but rather to the relationship between non-counseling professionals and those children and youths who may wish to discuss their family's marital state with a familiar adult. Such professionals include teachers in preschool, elementary and secondary grades, day care givers, child care providers in institutions and group homes, pediatric nurses, child life specialists, recreation therapists, youth workers, pediatricians, and those who serve as guardians ad litem.

*Category 2*—Mental health professionals who work in a counseling role with children.

*Category 3*—Mental health professionals who work in a counseling role with adults.

The emphasis in categories 2 and 3 is on the counseling role of an adult and on the therapeutic relationship with children or adults. The articles listed for categories 2 and 3 will be of interest to psychiatrists, psychologists, social workers, guidance counselors, family therapists, and others counseling divorcing parents or children of divorcing parents, single parents, or stepfamilies.

*Category 4*—Legal, medical, and clerical professionals who work in a direct service, but non-counseling role with adults.

This category is similar to category 1, but the focus is on adults. Category 4 is relevant to professionals in fields other than counseling and mental health who may be called upon to discuss an adult's divorce or give advice to an adult concerning divorce, custody, or child-rearing issues. Articles in category 4 will interest lawyers, clergy, pediatricians, obstetricians, or other medical personnel, and those concerned with work and family life in private industry. Parents frequently turn to these professionals for advice without necessarily assuming a therapeutic relationship with them.

The emphasis of the articles in categories 1 and 4 is on the issues faced by children and adults experiencing marital disruption rather than on the therapeutic interventions to be introduced. The range of topics includes: children's reactions to divorce, parent-child relationships, day-to-day living arrangements, visiting and custodial arrangements, activities for classroom teachers, and issues surrounding policies in educational or judicial institutions. Readings reflect a range of opinions on topics such as the mental health of children following a divorce, single or joint custody arrangements, the variety of relationships between the mental health consultant and the courts, and the role of the medical advisor concerning marital issues.

The emphasis in categories 2 and 3 is on various therapeutic interventions. Descriptions of individual counseling programs, support groups for children in schools, family therapy for new stepfamilies, and the effectiveness of different kinds of intervention are included in the references contained in categories 2 and 3. The articles included represent diverse opinions on issues as well as different theoretical approaches to the types of interventions that are needed. It is expected that some articles written for one audience of professionals may be of interest to other professionals and also some parents.

The category designations have been included as a useful guide for those who approach this subject from a particular perspective. It should be noted, however, that, in keeping with the interdisciplinary thrust of the bibliography, the approach to these categories has been inclusive rather than exclusive. Professionals may find much that is helpful in materials originally written in another discipline. Thus, for example, an article on the effectiveness of a therapy group for children would be noted in category 2, those counseling children. If the group were school-based, category 1 would be added so that teachers might read about the usefulness of such groups in their schools even though they would not run the group.

This bibliography was compiled in Boston during 1981. The author is grateful to staff members at the Wheelock College Library and Cary Memorial Library in Lexington for allowing use of their excellent resource material.

Extensive research was done by Debra Lande while she was a graduate student at Wheelock College. Additional help was provided by Jan Saks. Inspiration for this project was provided by Cliff Baden, Director of Continuing Education at Wheelock, and Frances Litman, Director of the Center for Parenting Studies. The staff in Continuing Education typed faithfully through sun and snow. Finally, cheerful support by my husband and children sustained me throughout this work.

# THE BIBLIOGRAPHY

1.  Abarbanel, Alice. "Shared Parenting after Separa-
    tion and Divorce: A Study of Joint Custody."
    *American Journal of Orthopsychiatry*, 49 (April
    1979): 320-29.

    The report of a study of four families in which
    divorced parents have maintained joint custody of
    their children suggests that this arrangement works
    well under certain conditions. Components of a
    successful joint custody arrangement are considered
    and limitations are discussed. See also entries
    2, 5, and 7.
    Categories 1, 3, and 4.

2.  Ahrons, Constance. "Joint Custody Arrangements in
    the Postdivorce Family." *Journal of Divorce*, 3
    (Spring 1980): 189-205.

    Investigates relationships of joint-custody par-
    ents and the advantages and complications associ-
    ated with their custodial arrangements. The author
    reports co-parenting led to shared responsibility,
    which reduced conflict between ex-spouses, increased
    resources for each other and the child, and allowed
    continued satisfaction in parenting. See also
    entries 1, 48, and 57.
    Category 4.

3.  Alexander, Sharon J. "Influential Factors on Di-
    vorced Parents in Determining Visitation Arrange-
    ments." *Journal of Divorce*, 3 (Spring 1980):
    223-39.

Investigates the so-called "best interests" stan-
dards for determining visitation arrangements. It
compares the best interests of the visiting parent,
child, custodial parent, and parental relationship.
Author reports that the interests of the child and
of the visiting parent are significantly more important than the custodial parent's best interests
and personal relationships between parents. See
also entries 14, 95, and 135.
Categories 3 and 4.

4.    ————. "Protecting the Child's Rights in Custody
      Cases." *Family Coordinator*, 26 (October 1977):
      377-82.

Argues that legislation to protect the rights
of the children in custody cases is needed for
assisting both parents and courts. Guidelines
that reflect the level of the parents' legal involvement is advocated: when parents choose mediation, a specialist in child custody is appointed
to educate and assist in decision making; when
parents choose litigation, counsel is appointed
to represent the child.
Categories 3 and 4.

5.    Allers, Robert. "Helping Children Understand
      Divorce." *Today's Education*, 69 (November-
      December 1980): 24GS-27GS.

Identifies behavior that can alert classroom
teachers to possible family stress, and suggests
classroom discussion and other activities teachers
can plan to help children understand their own
feelings about their parents' divorce. See also
entries 19, 27, 34, 118, and 146.
Category 1.

6.  Anderson, Hilary. "Children of Divorce." *Journal
    of Clinical Child Psychology*, 6 (Summer 1977):
    41-44.

    Describes the organization and work of CHILD
    (Children Helped in Litigated Divorce), which seeks
    to explore and remediate the negative effects of
    divorce on children. Its five basic objectives are:
    (1) public awareness; (2) parental awareness; (3)
    children's awareness; (4) children's protection;
    and (5) preservation of the family unit. Several
    similar projects conducted across the country,
    which include referral systems and interactions to
    establish family court systems, are described.
    Categories 1, 2, 3, and 4.

7.  Atkin, Edith, and Estelle Ruben. *Part-Time Father:
    A Guide for the Divorced Father*. New York: Van-
    guard Press, 1976. 191 pp.

    About the separated or divorced father and his
    relationship to his children. Deals with the
    variety of problems a divorced father faces at
    different stages of his children's development from
    infancy through adolescence. Discusses different
    stages of divorce process, from the breakup of the
    family to the evolving relationship of father and
    child as both adjust to the situation. See also
    entry 133.
    Categories 1 and 4.

8.  Baden, Clifford, ed. *Children and Divorce: An
    Overview of Recent Research*. Boston: Wheelock
    College, Center for Parenting Studies, 1980.
    165 pp.

    Overview of research offered in papers from a
    1978 symposium on children and divorce, which
    brought together researchers and clinicians. Work
    by Hetherington, Wallerstein, Tessman, Weiss,

Solnit, Bronfenbrenner, and Keshet and Zill is included.
Categories 1, 2, and 4.


9.  ————. *Parenting After Divorce*. Boston: Wheelock
    College, Center for Parenting Studies, 1980.
    48 pp.

    Overview of issues faced by parents following
    divorce. Topics include single-parent experiences,
    mothers without custody, visiting fathers, joint
    custody, family forum as a form of therapy, and
    the mini-family in the stepfamily.
    Categories 1 and 4.


10. Beal, Edward W. "A Family Systems Perspective."
    *Journal of Social Issues*, 35 (Fall 1979): 140-
    54.

    Uses the concepts of family system theory and
    therapy to describe the changes and reworking of
    emotional attachments in families undergoing sepa-
    ration or divorce. Compares the management of re-
    directed affection and concern in families that
    have varied degrees of child focus. Considers
    family therapy in relation to these issues.
    Categories 2 and 3.


11. Benedek, Elissa P., and Richard S. Benedek. "Joint
    Custody: Solution or Illusion." *American Journal
    of Psychiatry*, 136 (December 1976): 1540-44.

    Explores the benefits and risks of joint custody.
    Benefits for parents include: continued relation-
    ship with each other, reduced responsibilities of
    child-rearing alone, avoidance of creating a winner
    or loser in a custody case. Benefits for children
    include: reinforced love of both parents, dual sex
    role models, and diminished need for fantasies about

non-custodial parent. Risks for parents include: guilt, feeling of betrayal of child, and cost of maintaining two homes geographically nearby and suited for child(ren). Risks for children include: inconsistency of rules, routines, and lifestyles, continued hostility between parents, and conflicts over loyalty. A risk for both parents and children is the latters' sense of not being "at home" in either establishment. Authors recommend further study on long- and short-term effects of a variety of custody plans so that appropriate arrangements can be made based on each situation. Categories 2, 3, and 4.

12.  Benedek, Richard S., and Elissa P. Benedek. "Children of Divorce:  Can We Meet Their Needs?" *Journal of Social Issues*, 35 (Fall 1979): 155-69.

Outlines some of the needs for support services of children of divorce, examines existing systems for the delivery of services, and assesses the extent to which the systems are meeting those needs. Authors conclude that existing services, public and private, are essentially inadequate, and describes the major characteristics of a model court-approved program designed to deal appropriately with the specific needs of the affected children.
Categories 1 and 4.

13.  ————. "Post Divorce Visitation:  A Child's Right." *Journal of American Academy of Child Psychiatry*, 16.

Argues that in most divorce cases it is in the best interests of the child to maintain contact with both parents. Some problems associated with visitation are examined. Authors believe that legal rights should be preserved and that courts, attorneys, and other interested persons should

make better use of clinical reports based on research in this area. Describes benefits that may
be derived from maintaining relationships between
children and noncustodial parents and offers suggestions for responding to visitation controver-
sies.
Category 2.

14.  Benedek, Richard, Robert L. Del Campo, and Elissa
     P. Benedek. "Michigan's Friends of the Court:
     Creative Programs for Children of Divorce."
     *The Family Coordinator*, 26 (October 1977):
     477-51.

     Description of Michigan's Friends of the Court
     system for handling divorce and family issues
     such as recommendations for child custody and sup-
     port, and visitation. Although the service is
     primarily concerned with enforcement and collec-
     tion of child support payments, the authors des-
     cribe its potential to provide counseling and
     other related human services.
     Categories 2, 3, and 4.

15.  Berg, Berthold, and Robert Kelly. "The Measured
     Self-Esteem of Children from Broken, Rejected
     and Accepted Families." *Journal of Divorce*,
     2 (Summer 1979): 363-69.

     Using Piers-Harris Children's Self-Concept
     Scale, authors find no evidence of lower self-
     esteem in children of divorced parents compared to
     those from intact families who live in an atmos-
     phere of acceptance. Children who grow up in in-
     tact families, but are made to feel rejected, are
     found to have by far the lowest level of self-
     esteem.
     Category 1.

16. Bernard, Jamine M. "Divorce and Young Children:
    Relationship in Transition." *Elementary School
    Guidance and Counseling*, 12 (February 1978):
    188-97.

    Discusses implications of divorce for the young
    child. Focuses on (1) the appropriateness of the
    Kubler-Ross grief model and (2) the importance of
    cognitive development stages in determining how
    to work with the younger child. Five specific
    differences between death and dying are discussed.
    The implications of Piaget's four periods for
    children's adjustment are examined. The author
    suggests ways counselors can help children deal
    with their feelings. See also entry 63.
    Categories 1 and 2.


17. Bledsoe, Eugene. "Divorce and Values Teaching."
    *Journal of Divorce*, 1 (Summer 1978): 371-79.

    Offers case examples and suggests activities
    and policies for teachers who wish to help students
    during the crisis of divorce. Focus is on high
    school-age students. See entries 27 and 34.
    Category 1.


18. Brandwein, Ruth A. "After Divorce: A Focus on
    Single Parent Families." *The Urban and Social
    Change Review*, 10 (Winter 1977): 21-25.

    Emphasizes the positive aspects of divorced
    and single-parent family life. Believes soci-
    etal attitudes and existing economic policies
    cause further family difficulties. Suggests that
    attitudinal change away from stigmatization of
    divorce is essential to increase public and pri-
    vate support for single-parent families.
    Categories 1, 2, and 3.

19.  Braun, Samuel J., and Dorothy M. Sang.  "When
     Parents Split."  *Day Care and Early Education*,
     4 (November-December 1976): 26-29.

     Examines the process of divorce from the point
     of view of the child, parents, and teacher.  Offers
     specific suggestions to teachers working with child-
     ren of divorce, including talking to children and
     parents, activities, and books to share.  See also
     entries 118 and 146.
     Category 1.


20.  Bronfenbrenner, Urie.  "The Changing American
     Family."  *AFL-CIO American Federationist*,
     (February 1977): 7-11.

     Reflects on changes in the family over the last
     25 years, particularly in parent-child interaction.
     With the increasing number of divorces, families
     in which both parents work, and fragmentation in
     society, author feels parent role has been re-
     placed by television, peer groups, and loneliness.
     Challenges reader to think of a new policy to sup-
     port families.  See also entry 8.
     Categories 1 and 4.


21.  Brown, B. Frank.  "A Study of the School Needs of
     Children with One-Parent Families."  *Phi Delta
     Kappan*, 61 (April 1980): 537-540.

     An interim report of school performance of over
     8,000 children from one-parent families.  Author
     discusses trends and makes some suggestions for
     changes in schools' policies to facilitate commu-
     nication with one-parent families.
     Category 1.


22.  Buxton, Martin.  "Applying the Guidelines of *Be-
     yond the Best Interest of the Child*."  *Child
     Psychiatry and Human Development*, 2 (Winter 1976):
     94-102.

Using three case histories, author supports
guidelines and legal psychiatric principles as
"applicable to all present-day custodial decision
making." Views *Beyond the Best Interest* as a
"landmark work in the field of preventative foren-
sic psychiatry" and endorses its notion of "least
detrimental available alternative guideline."
Acknowledges complexity of issues contained in
the book, but maintains respect for its policy
and strategy positions. Compare with entry 54.
Categories 2 and 4.

23. Cantor, Dorothy W. "School-Based Groups for
    Children of Divorce." *Journal of Divorce*,
    1 (Winter 1977): 183-87.

    Proposes the establishment within the schools
    of situation/transition groups to be led by school
    mental health personnel. The groups provide imme-
    diate crisis intervention and ongoing support to
    children of divorcing parents as a means of pre-
    venting the development of psychopathology. A
    ten-week program conducted at an elementary school
    is described, and evaluation of the results and
    future plans for the program are discussed. See
    also entry 63.
    Categories 1 and 2.

24. "Children of Divorce." *Journal of Social Issues*,
    35 (Fall 1979).

    Entire issue focuses on topic of children of
    divorce. Provides comprehensive overview of state
    of research and policy in this subject. See also
    entries 10, 12, 47, 53, 68, 73, 108, 140, and 175.
    Categories 1 and 4.

25. "Counseling Families." *Children Today*, 9 (Novem-
    ber-December 1980): 26.

Describes government publication, *Helping Youth and Families of Separation, Divorce, and Remarriage: A Program Manual.* Describes three models: family counseling model for families experiencing severe difficulties; educational model using a structured curriculum; and self-help model encouraging sharing feelings and information. Categories 2 and 3.

26.  Cox, Martha J., and Roger D. Cox. "Socialization of Young Children in the Divorced Family." *Journal of Research and Development in Education*, 13 (Fall 1979): 58-67.

Reports on Virginia study done with Mavis Hetherington. Presents findings on the impact of divorce on individuals, family interactions, and on children's social and intellectual development. Category 1.

27.  Damon, Parker. "When the Family Comes Apart: What School Can Do." *National Elementary Principal*, 59 (October 1979): 66-75.

Gives specific tips from a school principal to principals and teachers about activities and attitudes that schools can adopt to help families of divorce. Suggestions include changes in curriculum, school policy, parent outreach. Category 1 and 4.

28.  Dancy, Barbara L., and Paul J. Handal. "Perceived Family Climate of Black Adolescents: A Function of Parental Marital Status or Perceived Conflict." *Journal of Community Psychology*, 8 (July 1980): 208-14.

Using the family environment scale, examines real and ideal family climates as perceived by black adolescents from divorced and intact homes. Authors report that family climate was unrelated to parental marital status, but was significantly related to perceived conflict within the home. One of the few studies on black families and divorce. See also entry 165. Category 1.

29. DeFrain, John, and Rod Eirick. "Coping as Divorced Single Parents: A Comparative Study of Fathers and Mothers." *Family Relations*, 30 (April 1981): 265-73.

   Study of single parents on their perceptions of the divorce process, their feelings as single parents, child-rearing issues, children's feelings and behaviors, relations with ex-spouses. In responding to sixty-three questions, mothers and fathers differed significantly on only one: fathers were more inclined to seek a preferred position in their children's affections. Categories 1 and 4.

30. Derdeyn, Andre P. "Child Custody: A Reflection of Cultural Change." *Journal of Clinical Child Psychology*, 7 (Fall 1978): 169-73.

   Reviews alterations taking place in the legal system with regard to child custody, noting that the major changes are reflections of society's perceptions of adult sex roles. The recent advancement of women's equal rights has worked to women's advantage with regard to custody. Fathers are now being considered as having an equal right to custody, and mothers are being held to be equally responsible for child support. Concludes that professionals in the mental health field do well to prepare themselves for the tasks ahead in child custody consultation. Categories 2, 3, and 4.

31.  ────. "Children of Divorce:  Intervention in
     the Phase of Separating."  *Pediatrics*, 6.

     Recommends pediatricians give more expert guid-
     ance to parents in areas of child development.
     For example, highlights how pediatricians can
     help children and parents understand everyday in-
     fluences that lead children to establish fantasies,
     and thus perhaps reduce possible adverse effects
     of both reality and make-believe.  See also entry
     84.
     Categories 1 and 4.


32.  ────. "A Consideration of Legal Issues in Child
     Custody Contests:  Implications for Change."
     *Archives of General Psychiatry*, 33 (1976): 165-
     71.

     Reviews the criteria by which courts award cus-
     tody of children and determine visitation rights.
     A review of literature pertaining to the effects
     of divorce on children reveals an absence of the
     types of empirical studies that would be most
     effective in influencing the courts.  Suggests
     that the condition of children in the courts can
     be considerably improved by the involvement of
     child psychiatrists in consultation, education,
     and field research.
     Category 2.


33.  DeSimone-Luis, Judith, Katherine O'Mahoney, and
     Dennis Hunt.  "Children of Separation and
     Divorce:  Factors Influence Adjustment."
     *Journal of Divorce*, 3 (Fall 1979): 37-42.

     Study of the adjustment of children to parental
     separation and divorce in light of demographic
     factors.  Overall adjustment of children was
     measured by a behavior checklist completed by

parents. The profiles of maladjusted children in this sample came from families who reported a 50 percent drop in income immediately following parental separation. Maladjusted children were between ages six and nine at time of separation from one parent. The implications of these factors and their interactions are discussed. See also entries 40 and 53.
Categories 1 and 4.


34.   Drake, Charles T., and Daniel McDougall. "Effects of the Absence of a Father and other Male Models on the Development of Boy's Sex Roles." *Developmental Psychology*, 13 (September 1977): 537-38.

Study of the significant effects of father absence by divorce, separation, desertion, or jailing on sex-role orientations, preference, and adoption of seven- and eight-year-old boys. In all, fifty-eight second-grade boys, twenty-nine with fathers present and twenty-nine with fathers absent, were given a series of tests to compare the effects of father availability.
Category 2.


35.   Drake, Ellen. "Helping the School Cope with Children of Divorce." *Journal of Divorce*, 3 (Fall 1979): 69-75.

School-age children of divorce are considered to be a population at risk. The author maintains that school is an excellent resource for children who may manifest problems there but not at home. School personnel need to be aware of the common problems associated with divorce. Intervention methods are proposed.
Categories 1 and 2.

36.  Duberman, Lucille. *Reconstituted Family, a Study
     of Remarried Couples and their Children.* Chi-
     cago: Nelson-Hall, 1975. 133 pp., plus Appendix
     and Index.

     Report of a sociological study of parents who
     remarry focuses on how stepfamilies differ from
     traditional families. Relationships between hus-
     band and wife, stepparent and stepchild, and step-
     siblings are studied. Guidelines are described
     for future research considerations.
     Category 4.


37.  Duquette, Donald N. "Child Custody Decision-Making:
     The Lawyer-Behavioral Scientist Interface." *Jour-
     nal of Clinical Child Psychology*, 7 (Fall 1978):
     192-95.

     Discusses problems of the legal system in child
     custody cases and proposes two alternative modes
     for deciding custody disputes. Author argues
     that the adversarial process is unresponsive to
     the child's best interests. Two traditional roles
     of behavioral scientists are described: (1) wit-
     ness/consultant for the mother or father and (2)
     expert to the court in child custody decisions.
     Two alternative roles are proposed for behavioral
     scientists involving greater collaboration with
     lawyers: (1) team representation of the child by
     both a lawyer and a psychologist and (2) counsel-
     ing and mediation among all parties to a case.
     Categories 2 and 4.


38.  Effron, A.K. "Children and Divorce: Help from
     an Elementary School." *Social Casework*, 61
     (May 1980): 305-12.

     Describes short-term group work in an elementary
     school. Specific examples and directions are in-
     cluded on how it works. Preparing parents and

children for the group, role playing, and creative
writing within the group and projects success are
discussed.
Categories 1 and 2.


39.  Epstein, Robert D.  "The Rights of Children and
     Law:  The Role of the Child in the Divorce Ac-
     tion."  *Child Abuse and Neglect:  The Interna-
     tional Journal*, 1 (1977): 153-57.

     Based on his experiences as a practicing attor-
     ney, the author suggests that child abuse during
     divorce is more subtle than the typical violent
     form.  Due to lack of professional assistance and
     input from the child, decisions regarding custody
     and visitation place the child between the parents
     without providing any neutral, helpful support.
     Category 4.


40.  Espenshade, Thomas, J.  "The Economic Consequence
     of Divorce."  *Journal of Marriage and the Family*,
     41 (August 1979): 615-25.

     Examines the economic hardships that divorce
     entails.  Wives usually are awarded custody of
     children without commensurate financial support.
     Social and legal policies usually focus on income
     transfer and enforcement of child support.  This
     article is one of few that notes economic rather
     than psychological effects on family.  See also
     entries 33 and 53.
     Category 4.


41.  Falk, Phyllis.  "One Out of Five."  *National Ele-
     mentary School Principal*, 59 (October 1979):
     76-80.

     Interim report of results of a survey by Nation-
     al Committee for Citizens in Education on commu-
     nication between single parent and the schools.

One thousand single parents in forty-seven states
reported on school programs and policies helpful
to their needs, plus the attitudes and assumptions
they encountered from school personnel.
Category 1.


42.  Fassler, Joan.  *Helping Children Cope, Mastering
     Stress through Books and Stories.*  New York:
     Free Press, 1978.  155 pp.

     A child psychologist reviews contemporary
     children's literature to suggest how books and
     stories can be used to help children grow and
     reduce fears and anxieties, and to initiate open
     communication between children and adults.  Chap-
     ters entitled "Separation Experiences" and "Life-
     style Changes" are of particular interest.  Dis-
     cussion on how to use books is included in each
     chapter.
     Category 1.


43.  Felner, R.D., and S.S. Farber.  "Social Policy
     for Child Custody:  A Multidisciplinary Frame-
     work."  *American Journal of Orthopsychiatry*,
     50 (April 1980):  341-47.

     Discusses need for collaboration between mental
     health and legal professionals in the development
     of positive, supportive social policy for child-
     ren involved in custody disputes.  Reviews prog-
     ress to date and suggests future directions.  ﹍
     Refers to Goldstein et al. (entry 54) and Roman
     and Haddad (entry 129).
     Categories 2 and 4.


44.  Fine, Stuart.  "Children in Divorce, Custody and
     Access Situations:  The Contributions of the
     Mental Health Professional."  *Journal of Child
     Psychology and Psychiatry and Allied Disciplines*,
     21 (October 1980):  353-61.

Review of literature on the contribution of
mental health professionals to the well-being of
children of divorce. Topics include effects on
children as reported by Wallerstein and Kelly,
pre-divorce counseling including mediation, post-
divorce counseling, and custody conflicts with
guidelines by Benedek and Benedek.
Categories 1 and 2.

45. Formanek, Ruth, and Anita Gurian. *Why? Children's Questions, What They Mean and How to Answer Them.* Boston: Houghton Mifflin, 1980.
204 pp.

Using their knowledge, particularly cognitive
child development, two psychologists discuss how
to give appropriate answers to difficult questions,
according to child's age. The chapters on divorce
and remarriage are of particular interest.
Category 1.

46. Friedman, Henry J. "The Father's Parenting Experience in Divorce." *American Journal of Psychiatry,* 137 (October 1980): 1177-82.

Discusses the father-child relationship as it
is influenced by divorce. Psychiatrists are often
consulted by individuals considering divorce who
are concerned about its probable impact on their
children. Analyses of data gathered from the
psychiatric treatment of fathers during divorce
indicated that there can be positive changes in
their parental bonds as a result of increased
opportunities to relate to children in a conflict-
free atmosphere.
Category 3.

47. Fulton, Julie A. "Parental Reports of Children's
Post-Divorce Adjustment." *Journal of Social
Issues,* 35 (Fall 1979): 126-39.

Report of a study of 560 divorced parents who
were asked to assess the impact of divorce on
their children. Compares differences in perceptions of mother and of father, as well as describing mutual perception of children's distress.
Categories 1 and 4.

48.   Galper, Miriam. *Co-Parenting: A Source Book for
the Separated or Divorced Family*. Philadelphia:
Running Press, 1978. 150 pp.

The concept of co-parenting or shared custody
allows both parents equal responsibility for their
children while living apart. Author uses examples
from her own personal experience as well as from
other parents and opinions of selected professionals. The book offers a how-to approach that includes such topics as scheduling, financial relationship to the ex-spouse, some legal advice, possible problems that may be encountered and ways to
face them. See also entries 57, 126, and 129.
Categories 1, 3, and 4.

49.   Gardner, Richard A. "Children of Divorce:   Some
Legal and Psychological Considerations." *Journal of Clinical Child Psychology*, 7 (Summer
1977): 3-6.

Summary of psychological and legal issues that
warrant special attention by professionals involved with separated parents and their children.
Stresses the importance of the counselor's strict
neutrality regarding the divorce decision and includes discussion of mandatory versus voluntary
counseling; explanations to children; parental
criticism of one another; children's reactions
to the divorce; custody determination; legal and
social changes that could lessen the psychological trauma of divorce.
Categories 1, 2, and 4.

50. ———. *The Parents' Book About Divorce.*
New York: Doubleday & Company, 1977. 368 pp.

Author offers practical advice to parents on
common problems they face in terms of their children's reactions to separation and divorce. Topics discussed include decision to divorce and
day-to-day problems of living through the divorce.
Categories 1 and 4.


51. ———. *Psychotherapy with Children of Divorce.*
New York: Jason Aronson, 1976. 528 pp.

Advice to the professional helping children
and their divorcing parents. The author specifically refers to psychotherapy and other therapeutic interventions he uses in private practice.
Also included are chapters with advice to parents
on possible child-related problems subsequent to
the divorce, and the role of the therapist in
divorce litigation.
Categories 2 and 4.


52. ———. "Social, Legal, and Therapeutic Changes
that Should Lessen the Traumatic Effects of
Divorce on Children." *Journal of the American
Academy of Psychoanalysis*, 6 (April 1978):
231-47.

Focuses on specific changes to reduce traumatic
effects of divorce on children. Neutral therapists might aid in maintaining open mediation
between parents and supporting parents' willingness to change. Author suggests that lawyers
should be viewed as advisors, and mental health
professionals as consultants and advocates.
Categories 2, 3, and 4.


53. Glick, Paul C. "Children of Divorced Parents in
Demographic Perspective." *Journal of Social
Issues*, 35 (Fall 1979): 170-82.

Report of demographic changes having to do with
single-parent families and with children of divorced parents between 1960 and 1978. Projects
the number of children expected to be living with
single parents in 1990. Also presents social and
economic characteristics of divorced parents and
possible demographic consequences of these patterns.
See also entries 33 and 40.
Categories 1 and 4.

54. Goldstein, Joseph, Anna Freud, and Albert J.
    Solnit. *Beyond the Best Interest of the Child*.
    New York: Free Press, 1973. 189 pp.

    Based on psychological theories of the impor-
    tance of attachment, the authors believe the law
    has not been in the best interest of the child.
    Suggests specific ways to rewrite the laws, tak-
    ing into account psychological theories on the
    importance of attachment. The authors' views on
    the custodial parents' total decision-making pow-
    er have been considered controversial. See
    entries 22 and 151.
    Categories 1, 2, 3, and 4.

55. Goldstein, Marion Zucker. "Fathering -- A Neg-
    lected Activity." *American Journal of Psycho-
    analysis*, 37 (1977): 325-36.

    Discusses therapy with men, focusing on issues
    of their parent roles. Describes cases of mari-
    tal conflict or separation.
    Category 3.

56. Green, Barbara J. "Helping Children of Divorce:
    A Multimodel Approach." *Elementary School
    Guidance and Counseling*, 13 (October 1978):
    31-45.

    Describes an eight-session group counseling pro-
    gram for children based on an educational frame-

work geared to help them cope with the stress of
divorce. Author feels approach is applicable for
group work dealing with other problems.
Categories 1 and 2.


57.   Greif, Judith Brown.   "Fathers, Children, and
      Joint Custody."  *American Journal of Ortho-*
      *psychiatry*, 49 (April 1979): 311-319.

      Based on a survey of forty middle-class divorced
      fathers, focusing on their perceptions of their
      children.  Author argues that children of divorce,
      as children of intact families, need loving re-
      lationships with two parents and that joint cus-
      tody arrangements should be encouraged.  See
      also entries 1 and 2.
      Categories 1 and 4.


58.   Grollman, Earl A., ed.  *Explaining Divorce to*
      *Children*.  Boston: Beacon Press, 1969.

      A compilation of information and perspectives
      from authors in the fields of psychology, psychi-
      atry, sociology, law, and religion.  Offers in-
      formation and suggestions regarding the expla-
      nation of divorce to children and a description
      of circumstances surrounding divorce that may
      affect them.  One of the early books written on
      this subject; sections are still relevant.
      Categories 1 and 4.


59.   Grollman, Earl A., and Sharon H. Grollman.  "How
      to Tell Children about Divorce."  *Journal of*
      *Clinical Child Psychology*, 7 (Summer 1977):
      35-37.

      Suggests guidelines for telling children about
      parents' impending divorce.  Parents are urged to
      be honest, open, and straightforward; to provide
      nonverbal support; and to limit details to those

the child can comprehend. Possible reactions of
youngsters are examined, with recommendations for
dealing with them. Telling a child about divorce
provides an opportunity for significant sharing of
emotion.
Categories 1 and 2.


60. Grossman, Sharyn M., Judy Ann Shea, and Gerald
    R. Adams. "Effects of Parental Divorce During
    Early Childhood on Ego Development and Identity
    Formation of College Students." *Journal of
    Divorce*, 3 (Spring 1980): 263-72.

    Assesses level of ego development, locus of
    control, and identity achievement in 294 college
    students from intact, divorced, and divorced-re-
    married family backgrounds. Authors report that
    divorce backgrounds were not predictive of lower
    scores on the three measures. In fact, males
    from divorced families recorded higher ego-
    identity achievement scores than males from in-
    tact families or females from intact or divorced
    families. No evidence was found for the argu-
    ment that remarriage (stepparenting) may attenu-
    ate negative consequences of divorce on college
    students' development.
    Categories 2 and 4.


61. Grote, Douglas F., and Jeffrey Weinstein. "Joint
    Custody: A Viable and Ideal Alternative."
    *Journal of Divorce*, 1 (Fall 1977): 43-52.

    Authors advocate joint custody as a more viable,
    flexible, and responsible solution to changing
    needs of children and parents after divorce.
    They argue that the impact and influence of both
    parents are vital and promote more effective func-
    tioning of child and parents. Joint custody
    offers choice, open communication, and balanced
    continuity, reducing child's and parent's sense
    of loss, loyalty conflicts, and externally de-

fined personal involvement.
Category 4.


62. Guerney, Louise, and Lucy Jordan. "Children of
    Divorce, a Community Support Group." *Journal
    of Divorce*, 2 (Spring 1979): 283-294.

    Describes a six-week program for children of
    divorcing parents who met with volunteer group
    leaders. Purpose of group was to assist child-
    ren's adjustment to divorce with respect to their
    attitude toward, growth in, and acceptance by the
    community as a whole, not just in school or clinic
    settings.
    Categories 2 and 4.


63. Hammond, Janice M. "Children of Divorce: Impli-
    cations for Counselors." *The School Counselor*,
    27 (September 1979): 7-14.

    Discusses the results of a study involving 165
    children, which looked at differences in self-
    concept, school behavior, and attitudes between
    children of intact and divorced families. Speci-
    fic information was obtained from children of
    divorce on their perceptions of the positive and
    negative effects of divorce. Implications of
    these findings and suggestions for what counsel-
    ors can do to help are discussed. Included is a
    brief list of children's books on the topic of
    divorce. See also entry 23.
    Categories 1 and 2.


64. Henning, James S. "Child Advocacy in Adoption and
    Divorce Cases: Where is the Wisdom of Solomon
    when We Really Need It?" *Journal of Clinical
    Psychology*, 5 (Fall 1976): 50-53.

    Urges more active forensic participation by
    mental health professionals, and gives suggestions

on how qualified professionals can become more
active in (1) educating the court system about
the advantages of psychological intervention on
the child's behalf and (2) providing expert witnesses to minimize the residual effects of marital discord, separation, divorce, or adoption.
Categories 1, 2, and 4.

65.  Henning, James S., and J. Thomas Oldham.  "Child-
     ren of Divorce:  Legal and Psychological Crises."
     *Journal of Clinical Child Psychology*, 6 (Summer
     1977): 55-59.

     Reviews legal and psychological problems that
     arise during the different development stages of
     children in connection with divorce.  Suggests
     interventions to assist children's understanding
     of what is happening, and to modify court system
     in reviewing custody determinations based on pa-
     rental fitness and children's developmental
     stages.
     Categories 2 and 4.

66.  Herrman, Margaret S., Patrick C. McKenny, and
     Ruth E. Weber.  "Attorneys' Perceptions of
     Their Role in Divorce."  *Journal of Divorce*,
     2 (Spring 1979): 313-22.

     Discusses the traditional legal advocate/adver-
     sary role of attorneys and their less traditional
     legal counselor role.  Points out need to educate
     clients about long-term ramifications of divorce,
     its impact on children (e.g., child support,
     custody), and the familiarity of attorneys with
     related supported services (e.g., psychothera-
     peutic) to promote the emotional well-being of
     all involved parties during and after the stress
     of divorce.
     Categories 2 and 4.

67. Herzog, Elizabeth, and Cecelia E. Sudia. "Families Without Partners." *Childhood Education*, 48 (January 1972): 175-81.

   Reviews research up to 1972 of children in fatherless homes. Emphasis is on demolishing stereotypes about damage to boys. Offers a historic perspective of work in this field. Category 1.

68. Hess, Robert D., and Kathleen A. Camara. "Post-Divorce Family Relationships as Mediating Factors in the Consequences of Divorce for Children." *Journal of Social Issues*, 35 (Fall 1979): 79-96.

   Studies how the psychological structure of the post-divorce family can mitigate the impact of divorce on children. For divorced and intact groups combined, the relationships among family members appeared to be more potent influences on child behavior than marital status. The negative effects of divorce were greatly lessened when the child maintained a positive relationship with both parents. The relationship with the noncustodial parent (usually the father) was as important as that with the mother. Discusses implications for research and for public policy. Categories 2 and 4.

69. Hetherington, E. Mavis. "Divorce: A Child's Perspective." *American Psychologist*, 34 (October 1979): 851-58.

   Contends that much of the confusion in studying the impact of divorce on children has been the result of failure to view divorce as a process involving a series of events and changes in life circumstances rather than as a single event. Presents an overview of the course of divorce and

its potential impact on children, and uses research findings as a basis for describing the
process as it is experienced by the child. Since
the research on single-parent families headed by
fathers is meager, the article focuses primarily
on children in mother-headed households.
Categories 2 and 3.

70.  ———. "Effects of Father Absence on Personality
     Development in Adolescent Daughters." *Develop-
     mental Psychology*, 1 (November 1972): 313-26.

     Studies behavior observed in adolescent girls
     living with their mothers following death or di-
     vorce of fathers, compared with matched group of
     daughters in intact families. Represents early
     work of author on this topic.
     Categories 1 and 2.

71.  Hetherington, E. Mavis, and Ross D. Parke. *Con-
     temporary Readings in Child Psychology*. New
     York: McGraw-Hill Book Company, 1977. 441 pp.

     Papers reflecting recent and revised understand-
     ing about children and their development are pre-
     sented. The foci of traditional and contemporary
     socialization efforts are discussed. Included in
     some papers is a discussion of familial factors
     affecting socialization efforts such as divorce,
     changes in the family, father-child interaction,
     and alternate childrearing arrangements.
     Category 1.

72.  Hetherington, E. Mavis, M. Cox, and R. Cox.
     "The Aftermath of Divorce." In J.H. Stevens and
     Marilyn Mathews, eds. *Mother-Child, Father-Child
     Relations*. Washington, D.C.: National Association
     for the Education of Young Children, 1978.

Focuses on changes and stresses experienced by
family members, and factors related to alterations
in parent-child interaction in two years following
divorce. See also entries 73 and 74.
Category 1.

73. ———. "Divorced Fathers." *Family Coordinator*,
25 (October 1976): 417-28.

Presents results of a longitudinal study of
forty-eight divorced parents and their preschool
children, who were evaluated through observation,
interview, self-report, rating scales, and stan-
dardized test measures at two months, one year,
and two years following divorce with a matched
group of forty-eight intact families. The process of disruption, coping, and adjustment by
fathers to the crisis of divorce is examined.
See also entry 164.
Categories 1 and 3.

74. ———. "Play and Social Interaction in Children
Following Divorce." *Journal of Social Issues*,
35 (Fall 1979): 26-47.

Presents the results of a longitudinal study
of the effects of divorce on play and social
interaction of preschool children. In the first
year following divorce disruptions were found in
both areas. The play patterns of these children
were less socially and cognitively mature when
measured shortly after divorce. The adverse effects had largely disappeared for girls by two
years after divorce; however, the effects were
more intense and enduring for boys. Limitations
and rigidity in fantasy play were particularly
notable. See also entry 71.
Categories 1 and 2.

75. Hodges, William F., Ralph C. Wechsler, and
    Constance Ballantine. "Divorce and the Pre-
    school Child: Cumulative Stress." *Journal of
    Divorce*, 3 (Fall 1979): 55-66.

    Study of twenty-six preschool children from
    divorced homes and twenty-six from intact homes
    through parent reports, preschool teacher reports,
    and direct observation. Few statistically signi-
    ficant differences were obtained between the
    groups. Families with younger parents, limited
    financial resources, and high rates of geographic
    mobility were predictive of maladjustments in
    divorcing families. These same variables were not
    related to maladjustment for children from intact
    families.
    Category 1.

76. Horner, Catherine Townsend. *The Single-Parent
    Family in Children's Books*. Metuchen, N.J.:
    Scarecrow Press, 1978. 172 pp.

    Annotated bibliography on single-parent families
    with section on children's books on divorce.
    Introductory article on bibliotherapy is included.
    Category 1.

77. Hozman, Thomas, and Donald J. Froiland. "Children
    Forgotten in Divorce." *Personnel and Guidance
    Journal*, 55 (May 1977): 530-33.

    Specific case examples of elementary school-age
    children's responses to divorce, according to the
    authors' divorce model (see entry 78). Suggestions
    for counseling techniques in response to each case.
    See also entry 23.
    Category 2.

78. ———. "Families in Divorce: A Proposed Model
    for Counseling the Children." *Family Coordina-
    tor*, 25 (July 1976): 271-76.

Presents a model designed to facilitate counseling with preadolescent children whose parents
are experiencing a divorce. The model, based on
Kubler-Ross stages of denial, anger, bargaining,
depression, and acceptance, is followed by techniques used in helping the child work through
each phase of feelings regarding the divorce.
Category 2.

79. Irving, Howard H. *Divorce Mediation, a Rational*
    *Alternative to the Adversary System.* New York:
    Universe Books, 1980. 186 pp.

    The author, a family mediator and professor of
    social work, describes divorce mediation. Chap-
    ters include advice on child custody and shared
    parenting. Case studies are included.
    Category 4.

80. Jackson, Anna M., Nancy S. Warner, Ruth Hornbein,
    Nancy Nelson, and Elliot Fortescue. "Beyond the
    Best Interests of the Child Revisited: An Ap-
    proach to Custody Evaluations." *Journal of*
    *Divorce*, 3 (Spring 1980): 207-22.

    Describes an evaluative procedure for determin-
    ing custody arrangements developed at Colorado
    Children's Diagnostic Center, based on one-week
    assessment by a team. Evaluation examines parent-
    al attitudes, relationships with children, and
    placements that will provide continuity and most
    positive influences on children's growth and de-
    velopment. The C.D.C. evaluations are initiated
    by court order. See also entry 54.
    Categories 2 and 4.

81. Jacobson, Doris S. "The Impact of Marital Sepa-
    ration/Divorce on Children: Parent-Child Sepa-
    ration and Child Adjustment." *Journal of Divorce*,
    1 (Summer 1978): 341-60.

Examines the association between the child's
psychosocial adjustment and the amount of time
and activity spent with each parent after separation.  The sample consisted of thirty families
(with fifty-one children), all of whom had experienced parental separation within twelve
months prior to the research interview.  See also
entries 82 and 83.
Categories 2 and 4.


82.   ———.  "The Impact of Marital Separation/Divorce
      on Children.  II.  Interparent Hostility and
      Child Adjustment."  *Journal of Divorce*, 2
      (Fall 1978): 3-14.

      Study of the impact of marital separation or
      divorce on children with focus on the expression
      of interparental hostility experienced in the
      family prior to separation as well as during
      study.  Thirty families were studied.  Author
      found seven- to twelve-year-olds were particularly
      vulnerable to hostility between their parents.
      Implications for counseling parents and children
      prior to separation are discussed.  See also en-
      tries 81 and 83.
      Categories 2, 3, and 4.


83.   ———.  "Impact of Marital Separation/Divorce on
      Children.  III.  Parent-Child Communication and
      Child Adjustment and Regression Analysis of Find-
      ings from Overall Study."  *Journal of Divorce*,
      2 (Winter 1978): 175-94.

      Reports on parent-child communication to pre-
      pare children for parental separation.  Third of
      a series of articles based on 1978 study.  See
      also entries 81 and 82.
      Categories 1, 2, and 4.

84.  Jellinek, Michael, and Lois Slovik. "Current Concepts in Psychiatry: Divorce-Impact on Children." *New England Journal of Medicine*, 305 (September 1981): 557-60.

Review of psychiatric and related literature for physicians who may be called on to advise patients undergoing divorce. Authors suggest physicians should elicit brief marital history and, in cases where a child appears to be at risk of psychological harm, refer the family for evaluation and intervention. See also entry 31.
Categories 2 and 4.


85.  Jenkins, Richard L. "Maxims in Child Custody Cases." *Family Coordinator*, 26 (October 1977): 385-89.

A child psychiatrist describes six maxims that are an outgrowth of his experience as an expert witness in cases involving child custody. He emphasizes the importance of maintaining neutrality toward the parents so that the child's interests remain of primary importance.
Categories 2 and 4.


86.  Jenkins, Shirley. "Children of Divorce." *Children Today*, 7 (March-April 1978): 16-30; 48.

Reviews four areas that require policy decisions having to do with the issues of children and divorce: economic problems and child support; custody issues and court involvement; emotional problems and therapeutic intervention; and kinship patterns in step-relationships.
Categories 1 and 4.


87.  Johnson, W.D. "Establishing a National Center for the Study of Divorce." *Family Coordinator*, 26 (July 1977): 263-68.

Proposes the development of a national center
for the study of divorce to be a clearinghouse
of statistics and sponsor of research and education.  Author outlines proposed structure and
purpose.
Categories 1 and 4.


88.  *Journal of Clinical Child Psychology*, 6 (Summer
     1977).

     Entire issue devoted to "Divorce:  Its Impact
     upon Children and Youth."  Themes include effects
     of divorce on children; treatment approaches to
     the individual, to the group, and in the community;
     issues of non-custodial fathers; and remarriage and
     stepparents.  See also entries 6, 49, 57, 65, 95,
     99, 122, 125, 128, 130, 144, and 155.
     Categories 1, 2, 3, and 4.


89.  *Journal of Divorce*.  New York: Haworth Press,
     1977.

     Purpose of this journal is "to clarify and fur-
     ther interprofessional understanding of divorce
     and divorce behavior and thereby to improve thera-
     peutic, legal, and community treatment of those
     who are divorcing, those already divorced, and
     their families.  The journal is directed toward
     the needs of marriage and family counselors/thera-
     pists, matrimonial attorneys, and other profession-
     als involved with predivorce, divorcing, or
     divorced persons and their families."  Four issues
     per year, beginning Fall 1977.
     Categories 1, 2, 3, and 4.


90.  Kalter, Neil.  "Children of Divorce in an Outpa-
     tient Psychiatric Population."  *American Journal
     of Orthopsychiatry*, 47 (January 1977): 40-51.

Comparison of children of divorce and stepfamilies to children of intact families. Study
of outpatient population with attention to cli-
ents' age, sex, and specific presenting symptoms.
Findings revealed that out of 387 intake records,
children ot divorce constituted nearly one-third
of referrals and suffered a higher incidence of
antisocial, delinquent behavior, and aggression
toward parents. No significant differences
emerged between children of divorce living in
one-parent families and those living with stepparents.
Categories 2 and 3.


91.  Kanoy, Korrell, and Brent C. Miller. "Children's
     Impact on the Parental Decision to Divorce."
     *Family Relations*, 29 (July 1980); 308-15.

     Theoretical formulations and empirical evi-
     dence are considered in assessing children's
     impact on divorce, and a model conceptualizing
     these effects is presented. Indicates that in
     some instances children may facilitate the pa-
     rental decision to divorce. Implications for
     parents, family practitioners, and researchers
     are discussed.
     Category 3.


92.  Kaplan, Stuart L. "Structural Family Therapy
     for Children of Divorce: Case Reports."
     *Family Process*, 16 (March 1977): 75-83.

     Describes structural therapy techniques for
     treating families experiencing divorce in which
     a child is symptomatic. The child's behavior may
     be a response to stresses prior to or after the
     divorce. The family configurations considered
     are: mother, child, and maternal grandparents;
     overprotective mother and child; helpless and
     mildly neglectful mother; father; new family for-

mation; and couples who divorce and marry new
spouses.
Categories 2 and 3.


93.  Kargman, Marie Witkin. "A Court-Appointed Child
     Advocate (*Guardian ad Litem*) Reports on Her Role
     in Contested Child Custody Cases and Looks to-
     ward the Future." *Journal of Divorce*, 3 (Fall
     1979): 77-89.

     Discusses problems faced by the judicial system
     in determining satisfactory living arrangements
     for the child and proposes an advocate for every
     child.
     Categories 2, 3, and 4.


94.  Kelly, Joan B., and Judith A. Wallerstein. "Chil-
     dren of Divorce." *National Elementary Princi-
     pal*, 59 (October 1979): 51-58.

     Summary of the most common divorce-engendered
     feelings and concerns of the elementary school-
     age child based on findings of a five-year longi-
     tudinal study. Focuses on behaviors and responses
     observed in the school setting shortly after pa-
     rents separate. Considers the actual and poten-
     tial role of the school in providing support to
     these youngsters. See also entries 21, 41, 100,
     and 169.
     Categories 1 and 2.


95.  ――――. "Part-Time Parent, Part-Time Child:
     Visiting after Divorce." *Journal of Clinical
     Child Psychology*, 6 (Summer 1977): 51-54.

     Descriptions of patterns of visitation between
     noncustodial parents and children after divorce
     as studied in a five-year clinical research pro-
     ject investigating the experience and effects of

divorce on 131 children and adolescents.  Factors
associated with the divorcing process itself and
its effect on the divorcing parent influenced the
visiting pattern that evolved.  See also entries
3, 13, 94, and 169.
Categories 2 and 3.


96.  Keshet, Harry F., and Kristine Rosenthal.  "Father-
     ing after Marital Separation." *Social Work*, 23
     (January 1977): 11-18.

     Report of a study of separated or divorced fa-
     thers who remained fully involved in the upbring-
     ing of their children.  As they underwent the
     transition from married parent to single father
     these men reported that meeting the demands of
     child care contributed to their own stability
     and personal growth.  See also entry 46.
     Category 3.


97.  Keshet, Jamie Kelem.  "From Separation to Step-
     family, a Subsystem Analysis." *Journal of
     Family Issues*, 1 (December 1980): 517-32.

     Explores the subsystems of relationships within
     the stepfamily.  These are: the new couple system;
     the ex-spouse system(s); and the parent-child sub-
     system(s), either custodial or visiting parent.
     Author maintains that through an analysis of exist-
     ing subsystems that compete for limited resources,
     stepfamilies can acknowledge conflicts between and
     within subsystems and become more unified by re-
     defining boundaries.  See also entries 10 and 92.
     Categories 1 and 3.


98.  Kessler, Sheila.  *Divorce Counseling*.  Ann Arbor,
     Mich.: Eric Counseling and Personnel Services
     Information Center, 1981.  55 pp., 47 pp.,
     bibliography and references.

Brief overview of trends, ideas, and resources
for counselors in area of divorce. Focuses on
author's model of counseling, using structured
interventions and format to enable divorcing parents to "let go, communicate with former spouse,
help children work through their feelings of
divorce," and to mobilize social skills towards
forming new relationships.
Category 2.


99.  Kessler, Sheila, and Sylvia H. Bostwick. "Beyond
     Divorce: Coping Skills for Children." *Journal
     of Clinical Child Psychology*, 7 (Summer 1977):
     38-41.

     Description of a workshop model for 10- to 17-
     year old children whose families are going through
     divorce. The rationale, dynamics, and format for
     this support and skill-building group are outlined.
     The first half of the six-hour workship helps de-
     fine needs and problem areas of the participants,
     while the second half centers on specific communi-
     cation skills designed to help master problem
     areas.
     Categories 1 and 2.


100. Kohn, Sherwood Davidson. "Coping with Family
     Change." *National Elementary Principal*, 59
     (October 1979): 40-50.

     Discusses the responsibility of the school res-
     ponding to changing family structures, with speci-
     fic examples of what some principals, teachers,
     and counselors are doing. See also entries 21,
     41, and 94.
     Categories 1 and 2.


101. Kulka, Richard A., and Helen Weingarten. "The
     Long-Term Effects of Parental Divorce in Child-
     hood on Adult Adjustment." *Journal of Social
     Issues*, 35 (Fall 1979): 50-76.

Examination of relation between the experience
of parental divorce or separation prior to age
sixteen, and adult adjustment and psychological
functioning. Uses data from two national cross-
sectional surveys conducted nearly twenty years
apart. Concludes that contrary to much of the
literature and popular thought, these early experiences have, at most, a modest effect on adult
adjustment.
Categories 3 and 4.

102. Kurdek, Lawrence A., and Albert E. Siesky, Jr.
"Children's Perceptions of their Parents'
Divorce." *Journal of Divorce*, 3 (Summer 1980):
339-78.

Shows that older children defined divorce as
psychological, emotional separation, while younger
ones viewed it as physical separation. Despite
adjustments in areas of noncustodial parental
relationship and additional household responsibilities, children's general acceptance of status
of both parents, peer relationships, self-esteem,
and attitude toward marriage for themselves in
the future were positive.
Categories 1 and 2.

103. ———. "Divorced Single Parents' Perceptions of
Child-Related Problems." *Journal of Divorce*,
1 (Summer 1978): 361-69.

Problems of greatest concern identified by
single parents are discipline, behavior problems
resulting from the separation and following the
ex-spouse's visit, and for single mothers, the
lack of an available male model. Based on a
sample of seventy-three divorced parents who rated
severity of a variety of child-centered problems.
See also entries 102 and 104.
Categories 1 and 4.

104. ————. "An Interview Study of Parents' Percep-
     tions of their Children's Reactions and Adjust-
     ments to Divorce." *Journal of Divorce*, 3 (Fall
     1979): 5-17.

     Interviews seventy-four parents about the degree
     of conflict in the pre-separation period, their
     children's reactions to the news of separation
     and present attitude toward the divorce, and their
     own estimation of strengths their children acquired
     as a result of adjusting to divorce. Attention was
     also directed to the extent to which parents' res-
     ponses varied as a function of sex of custodial
     parent, sex and age of child, and length of parent-
     al separation. See also entries 102 and 103.
     Categories 1 and 4.


105. ————. "Sex Role Self-Concepts of Single Divorced
     Parents and Their Child." *Journal of Divorce*,
     3 (Spring 1980): 249-61.

     Reports on their study of seventy-four parents
     (see entry 104), focusing on sex role self-concept.
     Questions the prevailing view that boys reared in
     mother-headed families become feminized.
     Categories 1 and 2.


106. Lamb, Michael E. "The Effects of Divorce on
     Children's Personality Development." *Journal
     of Divorce*, 1 (Winter 1977): 163-72.

     Review of the literature to 1977 and criteria
     for evaluating effects of divorce on children's
     personality development and of custody arrange-
     ments. Age and sex of child, relative ability
     and willingness of parents to care for child, and
     nature of parent-child relationship before sepa-
     ration are weighed. Supports the ideas that di-
     vorce is a constructive solution when marriage is

failing, and that custody should not automatically
be awarded to mother.
Categories 1 and 4.

107. Levine, James A. *Who Will Raise the Children?
New Options for Fathers (and Mothers)*. Philadelphia: J.B. Lippincott Company, 1976. 192 pp.

Description of various situations involving
childrearing and men, such as the single man who
adopts children, the husband and wife who share
jobs and child-care, the divorced father with custody, and the house-husband. The focus is on
fatherhood, the role of the single parent, and in
particular, on fathers who consciously choose the
role of an active father.
Categories 1 and 4.

108. Levitan, Teresa E. "Children of Divorce: An
Introduction." *Journal of Social Issues*, 35
(Fall 1979): 1-25.

Brief review of the major approaches and findings of past research on children of divorce.
Questions for future research are presented. As
an introduction to this issue, the editor reviews
some of the most current research findings on the
effects of divorce on children and describes some
of the complex issues and difficult problems of
research in this area.
Categories 1 and 2.

109. Lewis, Karen Gail. "Children of Lesbians: Their
Point of View." *Social Work*, 25 (May 1980):
198-203.

Interviews with twenty-one children aged nine
to twenty-six identified several major issues.
Problems experienced involved parents' divorce
and disclosure of mother's homosexuality. Prob-

lems between mother and child were secondary to
issue of children's respect for difficult step
she had taken.
Category 1.


110.   Lewis, Ken. "Single-Father Families: Who They
       Are and How They Fare." *Child Welfare*, 17
       (December 1978): 643-51.

       Reviews the literature on single fathers and
       divorce. Overview of articles through 1977.
       Category 4.


111.   Lowenstein, Joyce S., and Elizabeth J. Koopman.
       "A Comparison of Self-Esteem between Boys
       Living with Single-Parent Mothers and Single-
       Parent Fathers." *Journal of Divorce*, 2 (Winter
       1978): 195-207.

       Investigation of self-esteem in boys aged nine
       to fourteen as related to sex and adjustment to
       the custodial parent, frequency of visitation of
       noncustodial parent, length of time child lived
       in single-parent home, and quality of relation-
       ship between parents. Results indicated no par-
       ticular differences in self-esteem in relation
       to: age of boys and/or sex of single parent, time
       living in single-parent home after one year, or
       relationship between parents. Noted significant
       difference when frequency of visits of noncusto-
       dial parent exceeded one per month, with self-
       esteem higher than when visits were less frequent.
       Categories 1 and 4.


112.   Luepnitz, Deborah A. "Which Aspects of Divorce
       Affect Children?" *Family Coordinator*, 28
       (January 1979): 79-85.

       Interview study of twenty-four college-age stu-
       dents whose parents had divorced before they were

sixteen years old. Questions focused on identi-
fying stressful times, specifically pre-divorce,
transition, or post-divorce. Identifies times of
stress and coping strategies employed by children.
This is a retrospective study of a nonclinical
population.
Categories 1 and 4.

113. Magid, Kenneth. "Children Facing Divorce: A
Treatment Program." *Personnel and Guidance
Journal*, 55 (May 1977): 534-36.

Describes a short-term counseling program
offered by an inter-disciplinary staff for parents
and children facing divorce. Goals and structure
of program are described. Specific suggestions
for counselors, teachers, and parent consultants
are listed.
Categories 1, 2, and 3.

114. Magrab, Phyllis. "For the Sake of the Children:
A Review of the Psychological Effects of Divorce."
*Journal of Divorce*, 1 (Spring 1978): 233-44.

Discusses how for the child, divorce may represent a sense of loss and failure in interperson-
al relationships, and be a prelude to a difficult
transition. Psychological effects cannot be
viewed in a unitary way. Discusses support systems particularly for primary parent to enhance
ability to help vulnerable child.
Categories 3 and 4.

115. Mason, Edward. "The Children of Separation and
Divorce." *Sightlines*, 11 (Spring 1978): 15-
19.

Includes an annotated list of films and items
from other media for children and parents about
divorce. Accompanying article discusses possible

programs and combinations to use in various set-
tings in schools and in the community. Author is
a psychiatrist, a filmmaker, and a director of the
Mental Health Training Film Program at Harvard
Medical School. He reviews more recent films in
*Community Mental Health Journal.*
Categories 1 and 4.


116.  McDermott, J.F. "Divorce and Its Psychiatric
      Sequelae in Children." *Archives of General
      Psychiatry*, 23 (November 1970): 421-27.

      An early article in this field often referred
      to in other publications.
      Category 2.


117.  McDermott, John F., Wen-Shing Tseng, Walter Char,
      and Chantis Fukunaga. "Child Custody Decision
      Making, the Search for Improvement." *Journal
      of American Academy of Child Psychiatry*, 17
      (Winter 1978): 104-16.

      Description of a new assessment method, called
      the Parent-Child Interaction test, for use by the
      child psychiatrist involved in child custody de-
      cisions. Experiences of its use by a family
      court are described. The historical development
      of custody criteria and an analysis of the working
      philosophy of a typical family court are described,
      including criteria customarily considered and prob-
      lems encountered in decision making.
      Categories 2 and 4.


118.  McLinn, Diane. "Helping Children Cope with Di-
      vorce." *Child Care Resources*, 5 (October 1981):
      1-4, 10.

      Describes children's reactions to parents' di-
      vorce with suggestions on how a day-care teacher
      can help. See also entry 19.
      Category 1.

119.  Myricks, Noel.  "The Equal Rights Amendment:
      Its Potential Impact on Family Life."  *Family
      Coordinator*, 26 (October 1977): 321-24.

      Discusses potential impact of equal rights
      amendment in context of certain areas of family
      life, such as alimony, child support, child cus-
      tody, property ownerships.  Written before ERA
      was defeated in 1982.
      Category 4.

120.  Nichols, Robert, and James Troester.  "Custody
      Evaluation:  An Alternative?"  *Family Coordi-
      nator*, 28 (July 1979): 399-407.

      Describes an approach to custody battles where-
      in parents are helped to negotiate and create
      their own custody and visitation arrangements.
      The process, its strengths and problems, and
      parents' evaluative comments are discussed.
      Categories 3 and 4.

121.  Parish, Thomas.  "The Relationship between Fac-
      tors Associated with Father Loss and Indivi-
      duals' Level of Moral Judgement."  *Adolescence*,
      15 (Winter 1980): 535-41.

      College students were tested on their levels
      of moral judgment based on a Defining Issues
      Test.  Depressed levels were found, particularly
      in females who had experienced father absence
      due to divorce during adolescence.
      Category 1.

122.  Parks, Ann.  "Children and Youth of Divorce in
      Parents Without Partners, Inc."  *Journal of
      Clinical Psychology*, 6 (Summer 1977): 44-48.

      Describes programs offered by Parents Without
      Partners for children and youths.  Surveys of

PWP members indicate that active involvement is
beneficial to children's adjustment as well as
their own.  Significant contact with others, formation of kinship network, and practical services
help all members in family.
Categories 1 and 4.

123.  Ramos, Suzanne. *The Complete Book of Child Cus-
      tody*. New York: G.P. Putnam's Sons, 1979.
      320 pp.

      A discussion of custody and its ramifications
      for children, written especially for parents and
      for professionals who might find it useful in
      their work with parents and children.  Describes
      possible child custody arrangements and case his-
      tories that illustrate why particular arrangements
      may be suited to certain situations.  Includes
      discussions concerning possible legal tie-ups,
      problems particular to various custody arrange-
      ments, as well as life after the custody arrange-
      ment has been agreed on and enacted.
      Categories 1, 3, and 4.

124.  Ransom, Jane, Stephen Schlesinger, and Andre
      Derdeyn. "A Stepfamily in Formation." *American
      Journal of Orthopsychiatry*, 49 (January 1979):
      36-43.

      Advocates that increasing incidence of remarri-
      age requires mental health clinicians to develop
      skills for helping members of two families form a
      viable new family unit.  Proposes a three-stage
      model and discusses a case in which a child was
      focus of conflict in one family's progression
      through the stages.
      Categories 2 and 3.

125. Reinhard, David W. "The Reaction of Adolescent Boys and Girls to the Divorce of Their Parents." *Journal of Clinical Child Psychology*, 6 (Summer 1977): 21-23.

This study sought to determine in what ways, if any, the reactions of adolescent boys to the divorce of their parents differed from the reactions of adolescent girls. It also examined which reactions were most common among middle-class white adolescents. The results suggested no difference in reaction between these boys and girls, and the sample as a whole did not react to divorce in a particularly negative fashion. See entry 127. Category 1.

126. Ricci, Isolina. *Mom's House/Dad's House: Making Shared Custody Work*. New York: Macmillan Publishing Company, 1980. 270 pp.

A practical systematic guide on how to establish a working relationship between divorced parents to enable them to share custody and parenting. Covers stages of psychological distancing from ex-spouse, new relationships, and legal and financial negotiations, including several checklists. Book is based on author's experiences as a family therapist specializing in divorce, custody, single parenting, and remarriage. See also entry 48. Categories 1 and 4.

127. Richards, Arlene Kramer, and Irene Willis. "Effects on Adolescents of Living Arrangements Following Parental Separation or Divorce." *Journal of Pediatric Psychology*, 2 (1977): 135-37.

Describes the types of living arrangements most commonly used by divorced families in terms of their psychological consequences for adolescents. A case is presented in which arrangements prevent-

ing normal adolescent development were altered
to allow for growth. Custody, visitation, and
child support provisions are seen as interrelated
but separable factors that can be altered only by
considering their effects as part of an arrangement for living. See also entry 125.
Categories 1 and 4.


128.  Rohrlich, John A., Ruth Ranier, Linda Berg-Cross,
      and Gary Berg-Cross. "The Effects of Divorce:
      A Research Review with a Developmental Perspec-
      tive." *Journal of Clinical Child Psychology*,
      6 (Summer 1977): 15-20.

      Reviews the research to date with an emphasis on
      how children of different ages are differentially
      affected by divorce. Preschool, early latency,
      later latency, and adolescent characteristics are
      described. Therapeutic implications are discussed.
      Categories 1 and 2.


129.  Roman, Mel, and William Haddad. *The Disposable
      Parent, the Case for Joint Custody*. New York:
      Penguin Books, 1978. 196 pp.

      The authors argue the value of joint custody,
      citing many studies and case histories. In the
      chapter "The Impact of Divorce on Families" they
      refer extensively to studies by Mavis Hetherington
      (entry 72) and Judith Wallerstein and Joan Kelly
      (entry 169). Chapter entitled "Joint Custody"
      argues against the book *Beyond the Best Interest
      of the Child* (entry 54).
      Categories 1 and 4.


130.  Rosen, Rhona. "Children of Divorce: What They
      Feel about Access and other Aspects of the Di-
      vorce Experience." *Journal of Clinical Child
      Psychology*, 6 (Summer 1977): 24-25.

Interview study of ninety-two children of divorce,
ages nine to twenty-eight years, in South Africa.
Questions asked about staying in unhappy family,
access arrangements, and other aspects of divorce.
Answers revealed parents' unhappy marriage arouses
more conflict than divorce itself and that free
access to noncustodial parent was highly valued.
Category 4.

131. ————. "Some Crucial Issues Concerning Children
of Divorce." *Journal of Divorce*, 3 (Fall 1979):
19–25.

Considers two aspects of a post-divorce situation affecting children, namely custody and access
arrangements. Author found no significant difference in adjustment of child, regardless of sex
of child or custodial parent. Free access to noncustodial parent was highly valued.
Categories 2 and 4.

132. Rosenbaum, Jean, and Veryl Rosenbaum. *Stepparenting*. Corte Madera, California: Chandler and
Sharp Publishing, 1977. 142 pp.

The authors, a husband-and-wife team of psychiatrist and psychoanalyst, draw on their professional
backgrounds as well as their own personal experiences of being stepparents and stepchildren.
Areas of discussion range from laying the foundation for the new relationship and continuing
through to the day-to-day experiences and expec-
tations of being a stepparent. One particularly
interesting and valuable chapter addresses the
issue of child development in relation to parenting from infancy through the adolescent years.
See also entry 160.
Categories 2 and 3.

133.  Rosenthal, Kristine M., and Harry F. Keshet.
      *Fathers Without Partners: A Study of Fathers*
      *and the Family after Marital Separation.*
      Totowa, N.J.: Rowman & Littlefield, 1981.
      162 pp., plus appendices.

      This study examines the lifestyles of separated
      fathers who maintain regular contact with their
      young children after marital separation. Focus
      is on child-care schedules one year after separa-
      tion, patterns of shared parenting, and effects
      of being an active parent on father's self-esteem.
      Includes many case studies from in-depth inter-
      views. See also entry 7.
      Categories 1 and 4.


134.  Rosenthal, Perihan Aral. "Sudden Disappearance
      of One Parent with Separation and Divorce: The
      Grief and Treatment of Preschool Children."
      *Journal of Divorce*, 3 (Fall 1979): 43-53.

      Reports on the sudden departure due to divorce
      of one parent, its pathological effect on young
      children and their consequent treatment. Rela-
      tionship with remaining parent is more signifi-
      cant than feelings surrounding loss of other pa-
      rent.
      Category 2.


135.  Rowlands, Peter. *Saturday Parent: A Book for*
      *Separated Families.* New York: Continuum Pub-
      lishing Corp., 1980. 141 pp.

      Focusing on the role of visiting parents, in-
      formation is gathered from interviews and the
      author's personal experience. Issues covered in-
      clude the value of visiting for children and pa-
      rents, helpful advice for making visits successful
      guidelines for short or long visits, and a dis-
      cussion of dating and/or remarriage. Summarizes

major issues and contains practical advice for
the visiting parent--father or mother.
Categories 3 and 4.

136. Rubin, Lisa D., and James H. Price. "Divorce
     and Its Effects on Children." *Journal of School
     Health*, 49 (December 1979): 552-56.

     Delineates stages of adjustment for children
     and adolescents trying to cope with their parents'
     divorce, and discusses the emotional processes in-
     volved with divorce itself. Recommendations are
     made to school personnel advising better ways to
     assist the needs of these children.
     Category 1.


137. Salk, Lee. "On the Custody Rights of Fathers in
     Divorce." *Journal of Clinical Child Psychology*,
     6 (Summer 1977): 49-50.

     Describes past and current judicial decisions
     of custody rights that have focused on the un-
     fitness of the father, and in which custody was
     almost always given to the mother. It is argued
     this policy has deprived children and fathers of
     their constitutional rights and has had negative
     psychological implications for everyone in the
     family. Concludes that custody should be decided
     by determining which parent is better able to meet
     the physical and emotional needs of the child.
     Categories 3 and 4.


138. ————. *What Every Child Would Like Parents to
     Know about Divorce*. New York: Harper & Row,
     1978. 149 pp.

     Author focuses on the concerns and feelings of
     both parents and the child experiencing the diffi-
     culties of divorce. In addition, questions and

problems have been included from Salk's consulta-
tions with patients. The reader is given practical, timely advice for helping the child of
divorce.
Categories 1 and 2.


139.   Santrock, John W. "Effects of Father Absence on
       Sex-Typed Behaviors in Male Children: Reason
       for the Absence and Age of Onset of the Absence."
       *Journal of Genetic Psychology*, 130 (March 1977):
       3-10.

       Studies the effects of father absence on sex-
       typed behaviors in male children. Reason for
       father absence (death or divorce) and age of
       child at onset of absence studied in fifth-grade
       boys in West Virginia. Extensive study of school
       behavior and family situation. Compare this to
       Hetherington study of preschoolers (entry 72).
       Category 2.


140.   Santrock, John W., and Richard Warshak. "Father
       Custody and Social Development in Boys and
       Girls." *Journal of Social Issues*, 35 (Fall
       1979): 112-25.

       Studies the effects of father custody on chil-
       dren's social development by comparing children
       whose fathers have been awarded custody, those
       whose mothers have been awarded custody, and
       others from intact families. The most intriguing
       findings suggest that children living with the
       parent of the opposite sex are less well adjusted
       than those living with the parent of the same sex.
       In both instances, however, authoritative parent-
       ing by the custodial parent was positively linked
       with the child's competent social behavior.
       Categories 1 and 4.

141. Saxe, David B. "Some Reflections on the Interface of Law and Psychiatry in Child Custody Cases." *Journal of Psychiatry and Law*, 3 (Winter 1975): 504-14.

Reviews psychiatric studies dealing with the effect of custody disposition, paying particular attention to certain legal proceedings where psychiatric testimony played a major role. Concludes that lawyers and psychiatrists must work together more closely to provide for best interests of children.
Categories 2 and 4.


142. Schlesinger, Benjamin, and Rubin Todres. "Motherless Families: An Increasing Societal Pattern." *Child Welfare*, 55 (September-October 1976): 553-58.

Survey of seventy-two Canadian father-headed families, examining the effect of the situation on children, family life, and father's social life. Urges more acceptance by society of this increasing phenomenon, especially in economic and legal changes to support fathers.
Category 4.


143. Schoyer, Nancy L. "Divorce and the Preschool Child." *Childhood Education*, 57 (September-October 1980): 2-7.

Discusses the emotional turmoil experienced by a child of divorce and the role of the teacher in providing the child with stability and understanding.
Category 1.

144.  Seagull, Arthur A., and Elizabeth A. Seagull.
      "The Non-Custodial Father's Relationship to
      His Child: Conflicts and Solutions." *Journal
      of Clinical Child Psychology*, 7 (Summer 1977):
      11-15.

      Discusses psychological problems of noncusto-
      dial fathers and impact these may have on rela-
      tionship with their children. Describes methods
      for easing transition for children to new rela-
      tionship and methods for dealing with problems
      of visiting. Other views on this topic discussed
      in entries 26, 72, and 164.
      Categories 2 and 3.

145.  Shinn, Marybeth. "Father Absence and Children's
      Cognitive Development." *Psychological Bulletin*,
      85 (January 1978): 295-324.

      Reviews detrimental effects of father absence
      on child's cognitive development based on IQ,
      achievement tests, and school performance. Find-
      ings suggest that financial hardship, high anxiety,
      and poor parent-child interaction lead to low per-
      formance among children in single-parent families.
      Considering the mother's (in)ability to compensate
      for absence of father, sex role identification
      appears insignificant. Suggests longitudinal
      studies to determine whether cognitive effects
      precede, accompany, or follow the father's absence.
      Category 2.

146.  Skeen, Patsy, and Patrick C. McKenry. "The
      Teacher's Role in Facilitating a Child's Adjust-
      ment to Divorce." *Young Children*, 35 (July
      1980): 3-12.

      Suggests specific things for teachers to do to
      help young children and parents adjust. Also
      reviews the literature on children, parents, and

schools in the area of divorce.  Includes a list of books for children and adults.  See also entry 27.
Category 1.

147.  Solow, Robert A., and Paul L. Adams.  "Custody by Agreement:  Child Psychiatrist as Child Advocate."  *Journal of Psychiatry and Law*, 5 (1977):  77-100.

Stresses psychiatric values over legal ones, and recommends that child psychiatrists participate in divorce and custody decisions as objective, nonadversarial experts.  Outlines a concrete divorce agreement that allows for mediation, change, and cooperation, as well as willingness of parents and children to undergo psychiatric evaluation and monitoring as circumstances warrant.
Category 3 and 4.

148.  Sonnenschein-Schneider, Mary, and Kay L. Baird.  "Group Counseling Children of Divorce in the Elementary Schools:  Understanding Process and Technique."  *Personnel and Guidance Journal*, 59 (October 1980):  88-91.

Describes a counseling session for elementary school-age groups of children of divorce in the schools.  Concrete directions for mechanics of group formation and realistic discussion on the nature of group process and group techniques geared to appropriate levels of cognitive development.
Categories 1 and 2.

149.  Sorosky, Arthur D.  "The Psychological Effects of Divorce on Adolescents."  *Adolescence*, 12 (Spring 1977):  123-36.

Reviews existing literature on psychological effects of divorce on adolescents, and includes observations by psychiatrist in an upper-middle-class suburb. Describes many variables depending on parental relationship to ex-spouse and the child's age and stage. Differentiates between divorce-related problems and conflicts common to normal adolescence.
Category 3.

150. Spain, Eugene. "Children of Divorce--A Forgotten Constituency." *Social Studies*, 72 (March-April 1981): 91-94.

Explores the negative effects of divorce on children and suggests that a restructuring of marriage and divorce laws (which would prohibit divorce in marriage with dependent children) might be valid in addressing this injustice against children.
Category 4.

151. Stack, Carole B. "Who Owns the Child? Divorce and Child Custody Decisions in Middle-Class Families." *Social Problems*, 23 (April 1976): 505-15.

Disputes premise of *Beyond the Best Interests of the Child* (entry 54). Argues for custody to be awarded to both parents unless the courts find overriding reasons why such an arrangement would not be in best interest of the child. Based on the need for continuing relationships, it seems reasonable to reinforce bond between child and both parents, where each is competent and willing to assume such responsibility. Explores the notion of co-custody, entitling the parent best suited at a particular time to assume physical custody, while the other parent is encouraged to maintain the relationship. Custody counselors

would guide parents and child at such times.
Categories 1 and 4.

152. Stuart, Irving R., and Lawrence E. Abt, eds.
     *Children of Separation and Divorce.* New York:
     Crossman Publishers, 1981. 300 pp.

     A collection of articles written by psychologists,
     lawyers, clergymen, and social workers treats im-
     pact on children of separation and divorce. Em-
     phasis is on how the children feel toward their
     parents, their own rights and duties and those of
     their parents, and their problems in school and
     larger society. See also entry 58.
     Categories 1 and 2.

153. Suarez, J.M. "Mental Health Interventions in
     Divorce Proceedings." *American Journal of
     Orthopsychiatry*, 48 (April 1978): 273-83.

     Advocates preventive and therapeutic programs
     in addition to the traditional diagnostic and
     evaluative services typically requested by the
     legal system or the mental health professionals.
     Describes implementation of a program by UCLA
     Section of Legal Psychiatry.
     Categories 2, 3, and 4.

154. Swerdlow, Edith L. "Mental Health Services
     Available to the Bench and Bar to Assist in
     Resolving Problems Relating to Custody and
     Visitation in Family Law Cases." *Journal of
     Clinical Child Psychology*, 7 (Fall 1978):
     174-77.

     Discussion of how custody and visitation rights
     can become the focus of parental feelings in the
     dissolution of a marriage. Mental health pro-
     fessionals are of service to the family and the
     court by gathering and evaluating information,

as expert witnesses, and as mediators. Educating
and counseling parents about the traumatic impact
of divorce should become mandatory in dissolving
families with children. The results of a survey
in the state of California are presented, and the
effects of a post-divorce clinic are reviewed.
Categories 3 and 4.


155.  Tessman, Lora Heims. *Children of Parting Parents.*
      New York: Jason Aronson, 1978.  604 pp.

      Describes how separation from a parent through
      death or divorce is experienced by the child.
      The author, a child psychotherapist, divides the
      book into three major sections: theoretical con-
      siderations of the period of parting and grief
      in childhood; description of encounters with pa-
      rents and children, often around custody issues;
      and suggestions on helping children cope. See
      also entries 8 and 50.
      Category 2.


156.  Thies, Jill Matthews. "Beyond Divorce:  The
      Impact of Remarriage on Children." *Journal of
      Clinical Child Psychology*, 6 (Summer 1977):
      59-61.

      Suggests that remarriage is a potential crisis
      event that parallels divorce in significant ways.
      Remarriage as well as divorce entails major struc-
      tural and relationship changes in the family and
      issues of loss and the negotiation of new and
      additional psychological complexities.
      Categories 2 and 3.


157.  Turner, Marcia C., Susan A. Tynan, and Steven Jay
      Gross. "Staying--or Splitting: What's Best
      for the Kids?" *International Journal of Family
      Counseling*, 6 (Spring 1978): 52-54.

Examines the four options a couple has on reach-
ing the conclusion that their present marriage is
at an end: staying together as they are "for the
children," divorcing with "Blame's the game," try-
ing a "rebuilt" marriage, or having a "victimless"
divorce.
Category 3.

158.  Victor, Ira, and Win Ann Winkler. *Fathers and
      Custody.* New York: Hawthorn Books, 1977.
      181 pp.

      Some of the questions explored by the authors
      of this book include: Who is the custodial father?
      Who is the father fighting for custody? What
      effect does a father-headed household have on
      children? Who is the joint-custodial father and
      how do his children manage living in two house-
      holds? How does society see these men and what
      does the future hold for them? Various custody
      arrangements are described in detail.
      Category 4.

159.  Visher, Emily B., and John S. Visher. "Common
      Problems of Stepparents and their Spouses."
      *American Journal of Orthopsychiatry*, 48 (April
      1978): 252-61.

      Describes four common myths that impede family
      functioning, with case examples to illustrate the
      points. Includes recommended interventions, par-
      ticularly the use of support groups.
      Categories 1, 2, and 3.

160.  ————. *Stepfamilies: A Guide to Working with
      Stepparents and Stepchildren.* New York:
      Brunner/Mazel, 1979. 280 pp.

      A comprehensive introduction for therapists

working with any member of a stepfamily. Initial
chapters focus on characteristics of stepfamilies,
followed by chapters on therapeutic interventions
with husbands, wives, and children. Individual,
group, and family therapies are discussed. Problems and needs of children in stepfamilies are
addressed. Authors are stepparents and in private, psychiatric practice. See also entry 132.
Categories 1, 2, and 3.

161. Walker, Libby, et al. "An Annotated Bibliography
     of the Remarried, the Living Together, and
     their Children." *Family Process*, 18 (June
     1979): 193-212.

     Bibliography of articles and books for remarried
     families, covering material to April 1978.
     Categories 1, 2, 3, and 4.

162. Wallerstein, Judith S., and Joan B. Kelly. "Child-
     ren and Divorce: A Review." *Social Work*, 24
     (November 1979): 468-74.

     Reviews the findings of a five-year longitudinal
     study of 131 children ages three to eighteen in
     sixty families in Marin County, California. Des-
     cribes the implications for practice, research,
     and social policy. Discusses emotional impact
     of divorce on children and adolescents. See also
     entries 94, 95, and 169.
     Categories 1, 2, 3, and 4.

163. ————. "Divorce Counseling: A Community Service
     for Families in the midst of Divorce." *American
     Journal of Orthopsychiatry*, 47 (January 1977):
     4-22.

     Presents a conceptual framework for the develop-
     ment of child centered, preventive clinical ser-
     vices for divorcing families. The structure and

components of an intervention service, including treatment strategies, successful interventions, failures, therapist's role, transference and countertransference responses, and professional dilemmas, are discussed based on the findings of the five-year Children of Divorce Project. Categories 1 and 2.

164. ————. "Effects of Divorce on the Visiting Father-Child Relationship." *American Journal of Psychiatry*, 137 (December 1980): 1534-39.

Discusses results of Marin County study (see entry 196), particularly focusing on father-child relationships in a visiting situation. Categories 1, 2, and 3.

165. ————. "The Effects of Parental Divorce: The Adolescent Experience." In E. James Anthony and Cyrille Koupernik, eds. *The Child and His Family: Children at Psychiatric Risk*, Vol III. New York: Wiley-Interscience, 1974. pp. 489-506.

Discusses the impact of divorce on twenty-one children, aged thirteen and older, as observed shortly after initial separation and one year later. Categories 1 and 2.

166. ————. "The Effects of Parental Divorce: Experiences of the Child in Early Latency." *American Journal of Orthopsychiatry*, 46 (January 1976): 20-32.

Discusses the impact of divorce on twenty-six children in early latency, as observed shortly after the initial parental separation and one year later. Categories 1 and 2.

167.    ————.  "The Effects of Parental Divorce:  Experi-
        ences of the Child in Later Latency."  *American
        Journal of Orthopsychiatry*, 46 (April 1976):
        256-69.

        Discusses the impact of divorce on thirty-one
        children in later latency, as observed shortly
        after the initial parental separation and one
        year later.
        Categories 1 and 2.


168.    ————.  "The Effects of Parental Divorce:
        Experiences of the Preschool Child."  *Journal
        of American Academy of Child Psychiatry*, 14
        (Autumn 1975): 600-16.

        Presents initial responses of all thirty-four
        preschool children to the parental separation
        and pending divorce, and turns to a fuller con-
        sideration of fifteen children (44 percent) who
        at the second checkpoint of the study appeared
        in significantly worsened psychological condition.
        Categories 1 and 2.


169.    ————.  *Surviving the Breakup:  How Children and
        Parents Cope with Divorce*.  New York: Basic
        Books, 1980.  313 pp.

        Comprehensive overview of results gathered from
        five-year study of children ages three to eight-
        een experiencing divorce in Marin County, Cali-
        fornia.  Children's reactions at different ages,
        changes in parent-child relationships, and impli-
        cations for therapeutic intervention are addressed.
        Many anecdotes are included.
        Categories 1, 2, 3, and 4.


170.    Weinglass, Janet, Kenneth Kressel, and Morton
        Deutsch.  "The Role of Clergy in Divorce:  An
        Exploratory Survey."  *Journal of Divorce*, 2
        (Fall 1978): 57-82.

Interviews with twenty-one members of the
clergy involved in assisting in divorce. They
offer their opinions about divorce and the concept
of their role, ranging from offering support and
making referrals to short-term, reality-based
counseling. See also entry 182.
Category 4.

171. Weisfeld, David, and Martin S. Laser. "Divorced
Parents in Family Therapy in a Residential Treatment Setting." *Family Process*, 16 (June 1977):
229-36.

Evaluates the workings of a program in which
divorced parents are required to participate together in the family therapy of their child who
has been placed in a residential treatment center.
This therapy contributed to elimination of recidi-
vism and, according to follow-up reports, to significant and sustained improvement in the child's
functioning in school, home, and community activities.
Categories 1 and 4.

172. Weiss, Robert S. "The Emotional Impact of Marital Separation." *Journal of Social Issues*,
32 (Winter 1976): 135-45.

Describes the stages of grief an adult experiences while undergoing the transition from marriage to divorce. Addresses particularly the per-
sistence of the marital bond; responses to loss
of attachment, particularly anger; and management
of ambivalence. Based on author's extensive work
with separating adults.
Categories 1, 3, and 4.

173. ———. "Going it Alone." *National Elementary
Principal*, 59 (October 1979): 14-25.

Discusses problems of single parents, child
care, finances, and overloaded responsibility.
See also entry 174.
Categories 1 and 4.


174. ————. *Going It Alone: The Family Life and
Social Situations of the Single Parent.* New
York: Basic Books, 1979.  303 pp.

Through interviews the author studied both the
social situation and the family life of the man
or woman parenting alone.  Topics discussed included the day-to-day existence of being a single
parent, such as managing a household and raising
the children unpartnered.  In addition, the single
parent's need for a life outside of the home is
recognized and discussed.
Categories 1 and 4.


175. ————. "Growing Up a Little Faster: The Experience of Growing Up in a Single-Parent Household."
*Journal of Social Issues*, 35 (Fall 1979):
97-111.

Proposes a theory of the structure and functioning of a single-parent household as being without
the hierarchy usually present in two-parent families.  Based on interviews with parents and adolescents, managerial responsibilities are shared more
equally, which may foster early maturity in adolescents.
Categories 1 and 4.


176. ————. *Marital Separation.* New York: Basic
Books, 1975.  334 pp.

Explores why separations occur, discusses the
emotional ramifications caused by separation, and
looks at the various aspects involved in relation-

ships among separating partners, relatives, and friends. Discussion of the possible effects and/or problems children experience through the separation. The author drew on his own experience as well as those of others who experienced marital separation. See also entry 208.
Categories 1 and 3.


177. Wheeler, Michael. *Divided Children: A Legal Guide for Divorcing Parents.* New York: W.W. Norton & Company, 1980. 216 pp.

Guide to custody law and the legal problems that parents confront, not just during divorce but in the years that follow. This is a practical tool for parents who must agree on a custody arrangement. Questions and concerns addressed include reasonable visitation rights, agreeing on the right amount of child support, and deciding what type of custody arrangement to use. Author is a lawyer who advises parents.
Category 4.


178. "When the Family Comes Apart: What Schools Need to Know." *National Elementary Principal*, 59 (October 1979).

Entire issue devoted to children and divorce. See entries 27, 41, 94, 100, and 173.
Category 1.


179. Wilkinson, Gary S., and Robert T. Bleck. "Children's Divorce Groups." *Elementary School Guidance and Counseling*, 2 (February 1977): 205-13.

Outlines a strategy by which elementary schools can provide group counseling for children of divorce. Describes four goals focusing on child's understanding of situations. Concludes that

short-term group counseling is an acceptable means
of dealing with this particular developmental crisis in an elementary school setting.
Categories 1 and 2.


180.  Woody, J.D.  "Preventive Intervention for Child-
      ren of Divorce."  *Social Casework*, 59 (November
      1978): 537-44.

      Reviews research on children's reaction to di-
      vorce and the ability of parents to intervene.
      Suggests mental health professionals collaborate
      with the legal community to work on preventive
      intervention.
      Categories 1, 2, and 4.


181.  Young, David.  "A Court-Mandated Workshop for
      Adolescent Children of Divorcing Parents:  A
      Program Evaluation."  *Adolescence*, 15 (Winter
      1980): 763-74.

      Describes and evaluates a pre-divorce workshop
      established by a county court for adolescents.
      Discusses problems in running a workshop and in
      overcoming resistence.  At the end a majority of
      the adolescents judged the workshop helpful.
      Categories 2 and 4.


182.  Young, James J.  "Divorce in Contemporary Church
      and Society."  *Urban and Social Change Review*,
      10 (Winter 1977): 26-27.

      Suggests that church-sponsored divorce groups
      could provide people with a setting in which
      they could learn some of the skills necessary for
      a satisfying marriage.  In addition, it is pro-
      posed that church leaders support the kind of
      broad social strategies that will alleviate some
      of the conditions (poverty, unemployment, poor
      schools, and poor emotional and physical health

care) that tear marriages apart.  See also entry 170.
Categories 3 and 4.

# CATEGORIES

Numbers refer to entries, not pages.


*Category 1--Teachers and others who give direct service in a non-counseling role to children:*

1, 5, 6, 7, 8, 9, 13, 15, 16, 17, 18, 19, 20, 21,
23, 24, 26, 27, 28, 29, 31, 33, 35, 38, 41, 42,
44, 45, 47, 48, 49, 50, 53, 54, 56, 57, 58, 59, 63,
64, 67, 70, 71, 72, 73, 74, 75, 76, 83, 86, 87, 88,
89, 94, 97, 99, 100, 102, 103, 104, 105, 106, 107,
108, 109, 111, 112, 113, 115, 118, 121, 122, 123, 125,
126, 127, 128, 129, 133, 136, 138, 140, 143, 146,
148, 151, 152, 160, 161, 162, 163, 164, 165, 166,
167, 168, 171, 172, 173, 174, 175, 177, 178, 179.


*Category 2--Mental health professionals who work in a counseling role with children:*

6, 8, 10, 11, 13, 14, 16, 18, 22, 23, 25, 30, 32,
34, 35, 37, 38, 43, 44, 49, 51, 52, 54, 56, 59, 60,
62, 63, 64, 65, 66, 68, 69, 70, 74, 77, 78, 80, 81,
82, 83, 84, 85, 88, 89, 90, 92, 93, 94, 95, 98, 99,
100, 102, 105, 108, 113, 116, 117, 124, 128, 131,
132, 134, 138, 139, 141, 144, 145, 148, 149, 152,
153, 155, 156, 159, 160, 161, 162, 163, 164, 165,
166, 167, 168, 170, 178, 179, 180.

*Category 3--Mental health professionals who work in a counseling role with adults:*

1, 3, 4, 6, 10, 11, 14, 18, 25, 30, 46, 48, 49, 52, 54, 55, 69, 73, 82, 88, 89, 90, 91, 92, 93, 95, 96, 97, 101, 113, 114, 120, 123, 124, 132, 135, 137, 144, 147, 153, 154, 156, 157, 160, 161, 162, 164, 168, 173, 175, 181.

*Category 4--Legal, medical, and clerical professionals who work in a direct service, but non-counseling role with adults:*

1, 2, 3, 4, 6, 7, 8, 9, 11, 12, 14, 20, 22, 24, 27, 29, 30, 31, 33, 36, 39, 40, 43, 47, 48, 50, 51, 52, 53, 54, 57, 58, 60, 61, 62, 64, 65, 66, 68, 79, 80, 81, 82, 83, 84, 85, 86, 87, 88, 89, 93, 101, 103, 104, 106, 107, 110, 111, 112, 114, 115, 117, 119, 120, 122, 123, 126, 127, 129, 130, 131, 133, 135, 137, 140, 141, 142, 147, 150, 151, 153, 154, 158, 159, 161, 162, 164, 169, 171, 172, 174, 175, 176, 179, 180, 181.

PARENTS' BIBLIOGRAPHY

Despite the increasing incidence of divorce, there are
few bibliographies available for the lay public, particularly parents. This section includes books generally
available in public libraries and articles found in the
public press, magazines and newspapers, in the past few
years. Some books listed here, marked with an asterisk
(*), are annotated in the major section, indicating
their usefulness to professionals, particularly teachers
and lawyers. An overview of the knowledge on a specific
topic is best found in the articles. Frequently, studies that are entered in the major bibliography are re-
ferred to in these lay articles and are cross-referenced
accordingly. This list for parents should also be helpful for professionals who are novices in the field of
children and divorce and wish an easy introduction to
the issues involved.

\*      Atkin, Edith, and Estelle Ruben. *Part-Time Fa-
       ther: A Guide for the Divorced Father.*

       Cited above as entry 7.


183.   Berman, Claire. *Making It as a Stepparent: New
       Roles/New Rules.* New York: Doubleday & Company,
       1980. 190 pp.

       The author interviews remarried men and women and
       their children about their stepfamily situations.

Topics discussed include deciding which house to
live in, the weekend family, matters of discipline, his-and-hers stepfamily, money matters,
and becoming an instant parent. See also entries
184 and 213.


184.   Capaldi, Fredrick, and Barbara McRae. *Step-Fami-
lies: A Cooperative Responsibility*. New York:
New Viewpoints/Vision Books, 1979. 146 pp.

Tries to facilitate family unity between stepparents and stepchildren. Authors are family therapists specializing in working with stepfamilies
who discuss steps in process from original family
through single parent to stepfamily, including a
chapter on defining roles. Suggestions for specific actions to case examples are offered. See
also entries 183 and 213.


185.   Carro, Geraldine. "Children and Divorce." *Ladies
Home Journal*, 12 (December 1980): 80-81.

In a regular column on mothering, author cites
Wallerstein and Kelly study (entry 169) and sum-
marizes advice.


186.   Cassidy, Robert. *What Every Man Should Know
about Divorce*. Washington, D.C.: New Republic
Books, 1977. 246 pp.

Based on author's own experience as well as over
100 interviews with divorced men and professionals working with them, book offers straightforward advice for divorcing men on problems faced
in courts, on the job, with family and friends.
Chapter on children discusses Wallerstein and
Kelly study (entry 169).

187. "The Children of Divorce." *Newsweek*, February 11, 1980, pp. 58-66.

   Discussion of how far we are in understanding the impact of divorce on children. Briefly mentions signiticant research studies and several resources.

188. "The Children of Divorce: How to Cope with Their Psychological Problems." *Business Week*, April 2, 1979, pp. 202-04.

   In a personal business supplement article gives advice to parents on what to expect from children and the value of counseling.

189. Costello, Joan. "After Divorce: Making Visits Work." *Parents' Magazine*, 56 (February 1981): 88.

   Focuses on the needs of five- and six-year-olds, and offers guidelines for making visits work.

190. Despert, J. Louise. *Children of Divorce*. New York: Doubleday & Company, 1955. 298 pp.

   This book is a classic, one of the first ones written for the popular press. While some of the ideas are no longer applicable to the present generation, it nonetheless contains material that introduces the reader to the general problems of divorce.

191. "Dollar Decisions that Go with Divorce." *Changing Times*, 34 (June 1980): 51-53.

   Discussion of the major issues of dividing property and child support, and comments on other points to consider such as legal fees and unpaid bills. Considers tax implications. See follow-up article in June 1981 issue.  See also entry 229.

192.  Duffin, Sharyn R.  *Yours, Mine and Ours:  Tips
      for Stepparents.*  Washington, D.C.: U.S. Govern-
      ment Printing Office, 1978.  DHEW Publication
      No. (ADM) 78-676.  25 pp.

      Short pamphlet from the National Institute of
      Mental Health with tips on steps to take before
      remarriage to ease transition into a new family.
      Comments on common problems of stepparents with
      some suggestions for solutions.  Short resource
      list is included.  See also entry 215.

193.  Dullea, Georgia.  "Is Joint Custody Good for
      Children?"  *New York Times Magazine,* February
      3, 1980, pp. 32-40, 46.

      Review of the variety of opinions espoused by
      experts on joint custody as of 1980.  Quotes
      from Solnit, Roman, Salk, and Greif, all of whom
      have references in major parts of this biblio-
      graphy.

194.  Epstein, Joseph.  *Divorce in America:  Marriage
      in an Age of Possibility.*  New York: E.P. Dutton
      & Company, 1974.  318 pp.

      Combination of empirical studies, reviews and
      autobiographical data addressing, for the most
      part, experiences of the middle class.  The
      author discusses steps leading to divorce, the
      process of divorce itself, and life after divorce.
      Written with a strong bias towards the nuclear
      family, "despite all its flaws."

*     Fassler, Joan.  *Helping Children Cope, Mastering
      Stress through Books and Stories.*

Cited above as entry 42.

195.  Felker, Evelyn H.  *Raising Other People's Kids,*
      *Successful Child Rearing in the Restructured*
      *Family.*  Grand Rapids, Mich.: William Eerdman's
      Publishing Company, 1981.  162 pp.

      Aimed primarily at foster and adoptive parents,
      but some parts may be helpful for new stepparents.


*     Formanek, Ruth, and Anita Gurian.  *Why?  Child-*
      *ren's Questions, What They Mean and How to*
      *Answer Them.*

      Cited above as entry 45.


*     Galper, Miriam.  *Co-Parenting:  A Source Book for*
      *the Separated or Divorced Family.*

      Cited above as entry 48.


*     Gardner, Richard A.  *The Parents' Book About Di-*
      *vorce.*

      Cited above as entry 50.


196.  Gatley, Richard, and David Koulack.  *Single Fa-*
      *ther's Handbook:  A Guide for Separated and Di-*
      *vorced Fathers.*  New York: Anchor Books, 1979.

      Written by two separated fathers who are also
      psychologists, book provides some practical solu-
      tions to problems often encountered by separated
      fathers and assures them that the problems are
      not unique or insurmountable.  Emphasis is on
      relationships, becoming separated, and evolution
      of houseperson.  Authors give direct advice, spell-
      ing out alternative behaviors in specific examples.

197.  Geddes, Joan Bel. *How to Parent Alone: A Guide for Single Parents*. New York: Seabury Press, 1974.  293 pp.

      Parent care is the focus, with practical sugges-
      tions and thought-provoking ideas for the person
      who by choice or circumstances, is a single pa-
      rent.  Discussion is given to financial problems,
      increasing self-confidence, becoming assertive,
      and accepting capabilities and limitations to
      name a few areas.

198.  Gertz, Kathryn Rose.  "Children:  How to Minimize
      the Damage."  *Harper's Bazaar*, 3218 (January 1980):
      99 on.

      A section in a feature article on "Your Guide to
      Splitting Up," author refers to Wallerstein and
      Kelly study (entry 169).  Other sections are on
      topics of interest to adults, but do not focus
      on the child.

199.  Glass, Stuart.  "Questions All Children (Even
      From Happy Homes) Ask About Divorce."  *Good House-
      keeping*, (April 1980):  74 on.

      Straightforward answers about divorce, children,
      laws, and customs appropriate for school-age child-
      ren.

*     Grollman, Earl A., ed.  *Explaining Divorce to
      Children*.

      Cited above as entry 58.

200.  Grollman, Earl A., and Marjorie L. Grollman.
      *Living through Your Divorce*.  Boston: Beacon
      Press, 1978.  161 pp.

      A distillation of years of professional counsel-
      ing, the text is divided into five section, four
      of which deal with the process or steps of di-
      vorce.  The fifth chapter, "Becoming Whole Again,"
      offers a positive look at divorce.

201. Hawke, Sharryl, and David Knox. *One Child by Choice*. Englewood Cliffs, N.J.: Prentice-Hall, 1977. 227 pp.

The pros and cons of the only child, the myths attendant to "onliness," and the psychological effects on parent and child are discussed. Also, the authors look at the special problems of the single parent raising a single child, showing how to deal with the insecurity a child may experience as parents separate, remarry, or begin to develop sexual relationships with other adults.

202. Hope, Karol, and Nancy Young, eds. *Momma: The Sourcebook for Single Mothers*. New York: New American Library, 1976. 388 pp.

Anthology of ideas, helpful suggestions, and shared experiences from a group of single mothers. Experiences of divorce, single parenting, working, and remarriage are discussed. See also entry 231.

203. Hunt, Morton, and Bernice Hunt. *The Divorce Experience*. New York: McGraw-Hill Book Company, 1977. 268 pp.

Authors discuss the adult experience of divorce based on questionnaire survey of 984 adults, followed by 200 in-depth interviews of others. Certain chapters deal with the experiences of children as perceived by their parents.

204. "In Massachusetts: Divorced Kids." *Time*, July 11, 1979, pp. 6-7.

Describes groups for children and adolescents of divorced families in Lexington, Massachusetts.

* Irving, Howard H. *Divorce Mediation, a Rational Alternative to the Adversary System*.

Cited above as entry 79.


205.   Johnson, Nora. "Divorce Doesn't Ruin Children's
       Lives, But ...." *McCalls* (May 1981): 82-92.

       Author interviewed adults who experienced divorce
       as children and draws conclusions about helping
       children survive.


206.   Kalter, Suzy. *Instant Parent: A Guide for Step-
       parents, Part-Time Parents, and Grandparents.*
       New York: A & W Publishers, 1979.  268 pp.

       This book has many practical ideas for a person
       who has never been a parent.  Gives advice, such
       as how to tell if a child is sick.  Some parts
       refer to stepparents and part-time parents, such
       as how to negotiate visiting.


207.   Kosner, Alice. "Starting Over:  What Divorced
       Women Discover." *McCalls* (March 1979): 22-28.

       Report on a survey conducted by McCalls in which
       9,000 separated or divorced women responded and
       reported on their new lives, children, men, and
       jobs.


208.   Krantzler, Mel. *Creative Divorce, a New Opportu-
       nity for Personal Growth.*  New York: M. Evans and
       Company, 1973.  268 pp.

       Author draws from personal experience and pro-
       fessional work counseling other adults undergoing
       a divorce to describe the feelings and stages of
       the experience.  He gives advice to help move
       along to a positive growth experience.  Some sec-
       tions address relationships with children.  See
       also entry 176.


209.   ————. *Learning to Love Again.*  New York: Thomas
       Y. Crowell Company, 1977.  243 pp.

In-depth examination of the next stage of personal development after the immediate trauma of
divorce is over. Author discusses personal experiences as well as those of people who took
part in his "Learning to Love Again" seminars.
Four stages of learning to love again are identified and labeled. Also included is a chapter entitled "But What about the Children?" that discusses the role of stepparenting.


\*      Levine, James A. *Who Will Raise the Children?
New Options for Fathers (and Mothers)*.

Cited above as entry 107.


210.   Maddox, Brenda. *The Half-Parent: Living with
Other People's Children*. New York: M. Evans
& Company, 1975. 196 pp.

Author draws on interviews and her own experiences
as a stepparent. Topics include the first meeting
with the child/children, day-to-day living, new
babies, the role of grandparents, and coping with
the constant reminder of the absent parent. See
also entries 184 and 213.


211.   McFadden, Michael. *Bachelor Fatherhood: How to
Raise and Enjoy Your Children as a Single Parent*.
New York: Walker & Company, 1974. 154 pp.

Author draws on his experiences and those of
other single fathers and mothers. Includes practical advice on dealing with the divorce and
custody hearing, raising children, running a
household, cooking, and readjusting to life as
a bachelor in general. See also entry 7.


212.   Molinoff, Daniel D. "Life with Father." *New
York Times Magazine*, May 22, 1977, pp. 12-17.

Describes fathers who have exclusive custody of
their children.

213.  Noble, June, and William Noble. *How to Live
      with other People's Children.* New York: Hawthorn
      Books, 1977.  197 pp.

      Authors describe their own personal experiences
      as stepparents as well as those based on inter-
      views with other stepparents and with stepchild-
      ren coast to coast.  Topics addressed include
      preparation for becoming a stepparent, sugges-
      tions on how to handle particular problems that
      may arise, some legal background, and ideas that
      may improve the day-to-day living situation.
      Helpful practical advice.  See also entries 160,
      184, and 218.

214.  Norman, Michael.  "The New Extended Family:  Di-
      vorce Reshapes the American Household." *New York
      Times Magazine,* November 23, 1980, pp. 26 on.

      Describes three families extended through divorce
      and remarriage.

215.  *One Parent Families.* Washington, D.C.: U.S. Gov-
      ernment Printing Office, 1977.  DHEW Publication
      No. (OHD) 74-44.  20 pp.

      Four case histories of parents bringing up child-
      ren by themselves.  A variety of problems is dis-
      cussed, plus specific suggestions for getting
      help.

*     Ramos, Suzanne.  *The Complete Book of Child
      Custody.*

      Cited above as entry 123.

216.   Reingold, Carmel Berman. *Remarriage*. New York:
       Harper & Row, 1976.   171 pp.

       Interviews with many people involved in remarri-
       age on topics such as stepchildren, financial
       difficulties, effects on friends and family, and
       coping with the memory of the former mate.
       See also entry 228.


*       Ricci, Isolina. *Mom's House/Dad's House:
       Making Shared Custody Work*.

       Cited above as entry 126.


217.   Rice, F. Philip. *Step-Parenting*. Westport,
       Conn.: Condor Publishing Company, 1978.   187 pp.

       Written for stepparents by a marriage and divorce
       counselor, this book offers direct informal ad-
       vice for accepting one's own feelings and under-
       standing the children's, and gives solutions to
       specific communication problems.  See also en-
       tries 132 and 159.


*       Roman, Mel, and William Haddad. *The Disposable
       Parent, the Case for Joint Custody*.

       Cited above as entry 129.


218.   Roosevelt, Ruth, and Jeannette Lofas. *Living
       in Step*. New York: Stein & Day, 1976.   190 pp.

       Authors, both stepmothers, found good stepparent-
       ing a challenge.  They present an honest, realis-
       tic view that dispels the myth "I love you, I'll
       love your children."  Issues of stepparenting
       are introduced, with case histories and ideas
       for accepting the role effectively.  See also
       entries 132, 159, 213, and 217.

\*        Rosenbaum, Jean, and Veryl Rosenbaum. *Stepparent-
         ing.*

         Cited above as entry 132.


\*        Rosenthal, Kristine M., and Harry F. Keshet.
         *Fathers without Partners: A Study of Fathers
         and the Family after Marital Separation.*

         Cited above as entry 133.


219.     ————. "The Not-Quite Stepmother." *Psychology
         Today* (July 1978): 83.

         Report on how men with part-time custody of their
         children separate their parenting and social lives.
         Addresses the problems of dating and developing a
         stepmother relationship.


220.     Rowlands, Peter. *Saturday Parent: A Book for
         Separated Families.* New York: Continuum Publish-
         ing Corp., 1980. 141 pp.

         Focusing on the role of visiting parents, infor-
         mation is gathered from interviews and the author's
         personal experience. Issues covered include the
         value to children and parents of visiting, help-
         ful advice for making visits successful, guide-
         lines for short or long visits, and a discussion
         of dating and/or remarriage. This book covers
         major issues, but also is full of practical ad-
         vice for the visiting parent.


\*        Salk, Lee. *What Every Child Would Like Parents
         to Know about Divorce.*

         Cited above as entry 138.

221. Spilke, Francine Susan. *What about the Children?
A Divorced Parents' Handbook*. New York: Crown
Publishers, 1979. 80 pp.

     Offers parents support and concrete advice re-
     garding the many issues surrounding divorce.
     Topics include telling children about the di-
     vorce, visiting days, the working mother, and re-
     marriage. Accompanying this manual are two child-
     ren's books: *The Family That Changed: A Child's
     Book About Divorce* (entry 292) and *What about Me?
     Understanding Your Parents' Divorce*.

222. Spock, Benjamin. "How Divorced Parents Can Help
     Their Children." *Redbook Magazine* (July 1977):
     22-29.

     Discussion of ideas from Atkin and Ruben's book,
     *Part-Time Father* (entry 7). Famous pediatrician
     talks about divorce.

\*    Stuart, Irving R., and Lawrence E. Abt, eds.
     *Children of Separation and Divorce*.

     Cited above as entry 152.

223. Troyer, Warner. *Divorced Kids: Children of Di-
     vorce Speak Out and Give Advice to: Mothers,
     Fathers, Lovers* .... New York: Harcourt Brace
     Jovanovich, 1979. 175 pp.

     Canadian author interviewed hundreds of United
     States and Canadian children who presented their
     views of divorce. Reactions range from deep
     emotional trauma to resilience.

224. Turow, Rita. *Daddy Doesn't Live Here Anymore*.
     New York: Doubleday & Company, 1978. 215 pp.

Practical guide for parents who are dissolving their marriage. It describes how they can an- swer children's difficult questions and confront other problems that divorce can bring: avoiding competition with ex-spouse, coping with a differ- ent standard of living, preparing children for a parent's remarriage.

\*      Victor, Ira, and Win Ann Winkler. *Fathers and Custody.*

Cited above as entry 158.

\*      Visher, Emily, and John Visher. *Stepfamilies: A Guide to Working with Stepparents and Step- children.*

Cited above as entry 160.

225.  "Visiting after Divorce." *Parents' Magazine,* 56 (May 1981): 8.

Report on Wallerstein and Kelly's study (entry 169), finding no correlation between the fre- quency and regularity of visiting patterns after divorce and pre-separation father-child relation- ships.

226.  Wallerstein, Judith, and Joan Kelly. "Califor- nia's Children of Divorce." *Psychology Today* (January 1980): 67-76.

Report on five-year study of the effects of divorce on children. Adapted from *Surviving the Breakup* (entry 169).

\*      ————. *Surviving the Breakup: How Children and Parents Cope with Divorce.*

Cited above as entry 169.


\*      Weiss, Robert S.  *Going It Alone:  The Family
        Life and Social Situations of the Single Parent.*

        Cited above as entry 174.


\*      ———.  *Marital Separation.*

        Cited above as entry 176.


227.    Westoff, Leslie Aldridge.  *The Second Time Around:
        Remarriage in America.*  New York: Viking Press,
        1974.  170 pp.

        Author draws on personal experiences with re-
        marriage as well as those of the people she
        interviewed.  Topics addressed are reasons for
        remarriage, legal considerations, the "ex"-
        syndrome, money matters, and problems encountered
        in living with children in a remarried family.
        See also entry 216.


228.    "What You Should Know about Divorce Today."
        *Consumer Reports,* 46 (June 1981): 327-331.

        Discussion of financial and legal aspects of
        divorce, including update on family law and some
        tax consequences.  Includes sample separation
        agreement.  See also entry 191.


\*      Wheeler, Michael.  *Divided Children:  A Legal
        Guide for Divorcing Parents.*

        Cited above as entry 177.

229.  Wilkie, Jane. *The Divorced Woman's Handbook:*
      *An Outline for Starting the First Year Alone.*
      New York: William Morrow & Company, 1980.
      168 pp.

      Practical advice on finances, automobile care,
      record keeping, and the job market. Also in-
      cluded is a chapter giving attention to the
      children of divorce. This book offers the newly
      divorced woman assistance in regrouping and
      organizing her life by dealing with the day-to-
      day facts of living.

230.  Willison, Marilyn Murray. *Diary of a Divorced*
      *Mother.* New York: Wyden Books, 1980.  320 pp.

      Author describes her own experiences and feelings
      as a divorced mother. She approaches the topic
      from a very personal standpoint and although all
      readers will not have had the same experiences,
      generalizations can be drawn and comparisons
      made. Subjects included are dealing with old
      friends, raising the children, joining the job
      force, coping with holidays, and dating.

231.  Women in Transition, Inc. *Women in Transition:*
      *A Feminist Handbook on Separation and Divorce.*
      New York: Charles Scribner's Sons, 1975.  486 pp.

      Emotional, legal, and social support for women
      in transition, including advice and resource
      material, and stories, poems, and drawings re-
      flecting a variety of personal experiences.
      See also entry 202.

232.  Woolley, Persia. *Creative Survival for Single*
      *Mothers.* Millbrae, Calif.: Celestial Arts, 1975.
      144 pp.

Book directed to the single mother and the
various and complex aspects the role entails.
Drawing on personal experiences as a single mother,
author suggests that the task is not an easy one.
Practical advice on financial matters, job hunting,
meeting men, and understanding the children.


233.    ————. *The Custody Handbook*. New York: Summit
Books, 1979.  314 pp.

Step-by-step guide for divorcing parents looking
for alternatives in custody arrangements. Topics
discussed include deciding how to share, making
financial arrangements, how the courts function,
and how to work with lawyers and judges. Possible
custody arrangements are described, elaborated on,
and appraised. Includes checklists and sample
forms.


234.  Omitted.

# CHILDREN'S BIBLIOGRAPHY

This section contains books written for children, adolescents, and young adults. Just as in other sections of this volume, issues of concern to children of divorcing parents, single parents, and stepparents are addressed. Efforts have been made to find stories about families (entries 235 and 257) as well as books giving advice directed to children (entries 254 and 260). This section should be of particular use to teachers and to parents.

*Hints for Adults*

Before reading a book to a young child or suggesting a book to an older child, the adult should be familiar with the content. These books represent a variety of family lifestyles and types of living arrangements. Custodial mothers and fathers, dating parents, live-in friends of parents, as well as new stepfamilies are all included. Some adults may want to become more comfortable with their own feelings before being put in a situation of discussing with children an idea that is introduced in a book they recommend.

Effort has been made to choose books that reflect realistic feelings and include characters who are believable and portray emotions to which a child can relate. Some books suggest solutions to problems, others are open-ended, but "happy endings" are not necessary for entries to be included. Instead, most books show the child beginning to adjust, with some happy and some unhappy feelings, to the new family situation.

Parents, too, are portrayed as having a variety of
feelings and being realistic, not perfect. The inclusion of other adults--grandparents, teachers, adult
friends--is to be commended, since it may suggest that
the child can discuss new life situations with other
adults.

Finally, the book should reflect economic and
racial diversity. This is seldom found beyond the preschool level, as most books for children ages eleven
to fourteen years represent families in middle-income
situations.

The books in this section have been included to
represent an age range and variety of family arrangements and social and economic situations, or are written by well-known or well-beloved authors. Adults can
use them to initiate a discussion, to model their own
conversation, or to show the diversity of family arrangements found in our society today. Most are written directly for the child experiencing a marital
change, but some are appropriate to use with children
from intact families.

This author is particularly appreciative for the
excellent research done for this section by Debra Ann
Woolverton Lande while she was a graduate student at
Wheelock College.


235.   Adams, Florence. *Mushy Eggs*. New York: G.P.
       Putnam's Sons, 1973. Illustrated by Marilyn
       Hirsh. 32 pp. Ages 4-8.

       The parents of seven-year-old David and four-
       year-old Sam are divorced. The boys live with
       their mother in a Brooklyn brownstone but often
       stay with their father in New Jersey. This is
       a story of the boys' relationship with their
       baby sitter, Fanny, who is a much loved and sig-
       nificant part of their lives--she makes the best
       mushy eggs in the world. When Fanny decides to
       leave the family and return to Italy, the boys

experience grief, anger, and eventual acceptance
of the loss of a loved one.

236. Adler, C.S. *The Silver Coach*. New York: Coward,
McCann & Geoghegan, 1979. 122 pp. Ages 10-12.

Neither twelve-year-old Chris nor her six-year-
old sister looks forward to spending the summer
with their unknown grandmother in a remote wood-
land cabin, but the summer holds many surprises
for them, not the least of which is gradual
acceptance of their parents' divorce.

237. Alexander, Ann. *To Live a Lie*. New York:
Atheneum, 1975. Illustrated by Velma Ilsley.
165 pp. Ages 8-12.

Hurt by her parents' divorce, and living with
her father, Jennifer changes her name and tells
people her mother is dead. She is convinced
that her awkwardness and very presence were the
cause of her parents' divorce. She interprets
her mother's departure as total rejection.

238. Andrew, Jan. *Divorce and the American Family*.
New York: Franklin Watts. 1978. 119 pp. Ages
11 and up.

This book "takes a comprehensive look at current
knowledge about divorce and its effect on family
life." Discussion is given to divorce laws, remarriage, children of divorce, various lifestyles,
and the future of the family. A positive approach
shows that divorce can be a time to grow and
change rather than focusing on all the pain and
problems it can cause.

239.  Berger, Terry. *A Friend Can Help*. Milwaukee:
      Advance Learning Concepts, 1974. 32 pp. Ages
      5-8.

      A girl tells her friend about her parents' di-
      vorce, and feels better because of it. Simple
      text, with photographs of girls nine to ten
      years old.

240.  ────. *How Does It Feel When Your Parents Get
      Divorced?* New York: Julian Messner, 1977.
      Photographs by Miriam Shapiro. 62 pp. Ages 8-11.

      Discusses problems and emotions young people ex-
      perience when parents divorce, the family sepa-
      rates, and lifestyle changes. Although no real
      effort is made to show the means for coping with
      guilt, loneliness, and anger, these emotions are
      all accurately expressed.

241.  Blue, Rose. *A Month of Sundays*. New York:
      Franklin Watts, 1972. Illustrated by Ted Lewin.
      60 pp. Ages 9-11.

      Tells of the confusion felt by a child who is
      suddenly uprooted by parental separation and a
      drastic change in environment. The parents do
      a good job of convincing their son that the sepa-
      ration is not his fault.

242.  Blume, Judy. *It's Not the End of the World*.
      Scarsdale, N.Y.: Bradbury Press, 1972. 169 pp.
      Ages 10-12.

      Teenaged Jeff, angry about the divorce, runs away;
      the youngest child, Amy, is afraid that everyone
      will disappear; twelve-year-old Karen, the middle
      child, uses denial as her way of dealing with the
      divorce and concentrates on reuniting her parents.
      The parents in this story do not relate well to

their children, nor do they make any effort to clear up their children's confusion concerning the separation.

243. Boechman, Charles. *Surviving Your Parents' Divorce*. New York: Franklin Watts, 1980. 128 pp.

Straightforward advice to young adults about parents' divorce, single life, and possible remarriage. Topics covered include children's feelings, parents' fights, the process of divorce, and adjusting to new situations. There is a good list of resources.

244. Booher, Dianna Daniels. *Coping ... When Your Family Falls Apart*. New York: Julian Messner, 1979. 126 pp. Ages 9-12.

Practical guide discusses how to cope with the anger, anxieties, and fears the reader may be experiencing. Topics include getting through the initial stages of the divorce, changing family patterns, and stepfamilies.

245. Bradbury, Bianca. *Boy on the Run*. New York: Seabury Press, 1975. 126 pp. Ages 9-12.

Twelve-year-old Nick feels confined by his mother's overprotected love, so he decides to run away and survive on a lonely island. During the week on his own, he discovers a lot about himself and about how to cope with his family.

246. Cain, Barbara S., and Elissa P. Benedek. *What Would You Do? A Child's Book About Divorce*. Indianapolis: Saturday Evening Post Company, 1976. Illustrated by James Cummins. 42 pp. Ages 5-7.

Presents a series of common reactions shared by
many children regarding divorce. The authors
introduce and explore many feelings that are
often quite difficult for the child to articulate.

247.   Caines, Jeannette. *Daddy*. New York: Harper &
       Row, 1977. Illustrated by Ronald Himler. 32 pp.
       Ages 5-8.

       A child of separated parents describes the special
       activities she shares with her father on Saturdays.
       There are silly jokes and a visit with Dad's new
       friend, who laughs with them.

248.   Christopher, Matt. *The Fox Steals Home*. Boston:
       Little Brown & Company, 1978. Illustrated by
       Larry Johnson. 178 pp. Ages 8-10.

       Already troubled by his parents' divorce, Bobby
       Canfield is further distressed when he learns
       that his father, who has coached him in running
       bases, intends to move away.

249.   Clifton, Lucille. *Everett Anderson's 1. 2. 3.*
       New York: Holt, Rinehart & Winston, 1977.
       Illustrated by Ann Grifalcon. 26 pp. Ages 3-5.

       Everett Anderson ponders what you can do as one:
       have fun, also be lonesome. Two is his mother
       and himself. Three is Mr. Tom Perry who makes
       his mother smile and hum a lot, but it can be
       crowded when he comes to dinner.

250.   Corcoran, Barbara. *Hey, That's My Soul You're
       Stomping On*. New York: Atheneum, 1978. 122 pp.
       Ages 10-14.

       While her parents discuss possible divorce,
       sixteen-year-old Rachel spends the summer with

her grandparents and realizes everyone has problems, many more serious than hers.

251. Dexter, Pat Egan. *Arrow in the Wind.* New York:
Thomas Nelson, 1978. 160 pp. Ages 11-14.

As a result of his parent's separation and divorce, sixth-grader Benton Arrow grows more in-
dependent and forms a friendship with the school
bully. This is the story of a bad year in a boy's
life, of coping with an unpleasant reality, and
making the best of things.

252. Ewing, Kathryn. *A Private Matter.* New York:
Harcourt Brace Jovanovich, 1975. Illustrated
by Joan Sandin. 88 pp. Ages 8-11.

Nine-year-old Marcy becomes very attached to the
older man next door and pretends he is her father.
She learns a lot from him. When he moves away
she learns how to cope with loss.

253. Forrai, Maria S. *A Look at Divorce.* Minneapolis:
Lerner Publication Company, 1976. Text by
Margaret Sandford Pursell and photographs by
Maria S. Forrai. 36 pp. Ages 7-9.

Text and photographs describe problems faced by
the parents and children when a divorce occurs.
Topics explored include possible reasons for
divorce, changing family structures, and life in
general after the divorce. Emphasis is placed on
the fact that both parents still love the child.

254. Gardner, Richard A. *The Boys and Girls Book
about Divorce.* New York: Jason Aronson, 1970.
Illustrated by Alfred Lowenheim. 159 pp. Ages
7-14.

Deals with several issues that a child must face
when parents divorce, including who is to blame,
love between parent and child, anger and its uses,
and the fear of being left alone. Additional sections address the problems of getting along with
a divorced parent, dividing one's time between
parents who are living apart, and the difficulties of living with a stepfather or stepmother.
See also entries 50 and 51.

255.  Gilbert, Sara. *Trouble at Home*. New York: Loth-
      rop, Lee, & Shepard, 1981. 188 pp. Ages 11-14.

      For young people, this resource book is full of
      frank advice on getting help when faced with fa-
      mily problems. Chapters "When the Family Falls
      Apart" and "Divorce Is Only the Beginning" are
      appropriate for children faced with divorce and/
      or marriage.

256.  Glass, Stuart M. *A Divorce Dictionary: A Book
      for You and Your Children*. Boston: Little, Brown
      & Company, 1980. 71 pp. Ages 11 and up.

      Alphabetically arranged definitions and dis-
      cussions of a number of terms relating to divorce,
      from "abandonment" to "visitation rights."

257.  Goff, Beth. *Where Is Daddy? The Story of a
      Divorce*. Boston: Beacon Press, 1969. Illustrated
      by Susan Perl. 28 pp. Ages 4-8.

      This is the story of Janey, a preschooler. Fol-
      lowing her parents' divorce, Janey, her dog Funny,
      and her mother move in with her grandmother. Be-
      sides having to see her dad only on visits, Janey's
      mom gets a job and leaves her all day with her
      grandmother. The story handles the feelings of
      grief, confusion, and loneliness that follow di-
      vorce.

258. Green, Phyllis. *A New Mother for Martha*. New
     York: Human Sciences Press, 1978. Illustrated
     by Peggy Luks. 30 pp. Ages 5-8.

     Faced with her father's remarriage, a first-grader
     stubbornly insists that her dead mother will re-
     turn soon. A sensitive story that explores re-
     alistically the pain of letting go of someone you
     love. Coupled with this is the realization that
     it is possible and all right to love someone
     else--like a new stepmother.

259. Greene, Constance C. *A Girl Called Al*. New York:
     Viking Press, 1969. 126 pp. Ages 11-14.

     First in a series of books about Al who lives
     with her mother and hears from her father occa-
     sionally. Emphasis is on her developing friend-
     ship with another girl in the apartment house.

260. Grollman, Earl. *Talking about Divorce and Sepa-
     ration: A Dialogue Between Parent and Child*.
     Boston: Beacon Press, 1975. Illustrated by
     Alison Cann. 51 pp., plus 30-page parents'
     guide. Ages 4-7.

     A guide to helping young children of divorcing
     parents understand and accept the fact that
     their parents no longer live together. Parent
     reads this to the child. Includes a parents'
     guide, sources for further help, and bibliography
     for children and adults. See also entries 58
     and 59.

261. Harris, Mark Jonathan. *With a Wave of the Wand*.
     New York: Lothrop, Lee, & Shephard, 1980. 191
     pp. Ages 9-12.

     Almost twelve-year-old Marlee tries to adjust to
     her parents' separation and a move and tries ma-

gic to get them back together. In the end, she
faces painful reality and recognizes how she has
grown and accepted the situation.

262.  Hazen, Barbara Shook. *Two Homes to Live In:  A
      Child's-Eye View of Divorce*. New York: Human
      Sciences Press, 1978.  Illustrated by Peggy Luks.
      36 pp.  Ages 5-8.

      A little girl explains how she came to terms with
      her parents' divorce.  The author, writing from
      the child's point of view, acknowledges the pain
      that accompanies divorce while realistically
      portraying life after the divorce.  Themes dis-
      cussed include children's fear of causing the
      divorce, being unloved, and parental dating.

263.  Hunter, Evan. *Me and Mr. Stenner*.  Philadelphia:
      J.B. Lippincott Company, 1976.  157 pp.  Ages
      11-14.

      When her mother remarries, an eleven-year-old
      learns that she can grow to love her stepfather
      and still love her real father.

264.  Kalb, Jonah, and David Viscott. *What Every Kid
      Should Know*.  Boston: Houghton Mifflin, 1976.
      128 pp.  Ages 9-12.

      Discussion of the problems of growing up and
      suggestions on coping with various emotions,
      understanding oneself, getting along with others,
      and dealing with parents.  Final chapter focuses
      on parents divorcing.

265.  Kindred, Wendy. *Lucky Wilma*.  New York: Dial
      Press, 1973.  26 pp.  Ages 3-7.

Wilma spends Saturdays with her dad seeing museums, until one Saturday, when they decide to take a walk and discover the fun of just being together. Few words in the text; the pictures speak for themselves.

266. Klein, Norma. *Mom, the Wolfman and Me.* New York: Random House, 1972. 156 pp. Ages 11-14.

Brett's mother never got married, and most of the time they are both happy with their life together. Then when her mother begins dating, Brett has mixed feelings. Her reaction contrasts to that of her friend whose mother is eager to remarry. Brett adjusts gradually to living in a family with a mother and a father.

267. ————. *Taking Sides.* New York: Pantheon, 1974. 156 pp. Ages 10-14.

Twelve-year-old Nell adjusts to life with her father and five-year-old brother after her parents divorce. Weekends she spends with her mother in the country. The sudden illness of her father makes her worry about losing him, too. Klein's characters are honest and real—sometimes seemingly cruel, but capable of love and understanding.

268. LeShan, Eda. *What's Going to Happen to Me? When Parents Separate or Divorce.* New York: Four Winds Press, 1978. Illustrated by Richard Cuffari. 132 pp. Ages 9-12.

The author attempts to answer the many questions a child has about divorce. She explores the feelings of the child before, during, and after the separation.

269.  Lexau, Joan M. *Emily and the Klunky Baby and
      the Next-Door Dog.* New York: Dial Press, 1972.
      Illustrated by Martha Alexander. 40 pp. Ages
      4-8.

      Emily's bad day gets worse when, angry with her
      divorced mother, Emily takes her baby brother
      and runs away to live with Daddy. She and the
      baby end up going around the block and home again
      to mother, a big adventure. For young children,
      the story can offer first recognition of and
      insight into factors that can make people blind
      to others' views.

270.  ————. *Me Day.* New York: Dial Press, 1971.
      Illustrated by Robert Weaver. 28 pp. Ages 6-9.

      Rafer's parents are divorced and he misses his
      father, who no longer lives with the family.
      He is aware of some of the problems that caused
      his parents to quarrel and eventually divorce--
      his father's losing his job and his mother's
      having to support the family. But on Rafer's
      birthday what he wants most of all is to hear
      from his father.

271.  Lisker, Sonia O., and Leigh Dean. *Two Special
      Cards.* New York: Harcourt Brace Jovanovich,
      1976. Illustrations by Sonia O. Lisker.
      48 pp. Ages 4-7.

      Two children try to grow accustomed to their pa-
      rents' divorce. Careful not to neglect the more
      painful elements always a part of such a sever-
      ance, the authors have endeavored to emphasize
      the positive aspects, all told from a small
      child's viewpoint.

272.  List, Julie Autumn. *The Day the Loving Stopped:
      A Daughter's View of Her Parents' Divorce.* New
      York: Seaview Books, 1980. 214 pp. Young adults.

This biography by a twenty-three-year-old describes her memories of her childhood, her parents'
divorce when she was nine, and subsequent life of
parents, stepfamilies, and parents' friends.
The record of those days is captured through
journals and letters. Some young adult readers
may identify with the account.

273. Mann, Peggy. *My Dad Lives in a Downtown Hotel.*
New York: Doubleday and Company, 1973. Illustrated by Richard Cuffari. 92 pp. Ages 9-11.

From this first-person narrative, a reader can
gain insight into the bewilderment, anger, and
guild felt by a child confronted with family
separation. The story also describes the an-
guish felt by parents.

274. Mayle, Peter. *Divorce Can Happen to the Nicest
People.* New York: Macmillan Publishing Company,
1979. Illustrated by Arthur Robins. 28 pp.
Ages 9-12.

This book is designed to help parents explain
the divorce to children through simple language
and cartoon illustrations. It describes feelings
one may have about marriage, divorce, dating,
guilt, and getting help.

275. Mazer, Norma. *I Trissy.* New York: Delacorte
Press, 1971. 150 pp. Ages 7-11.

Eleven-year-old Trissy behaves angrily toward
everyone because she wants to reunite her divorced
parents. She has problems with her parents'
dating other people. Eventually, her actions
are no longer merely embarassing as she becomes
seriously destructive to herself and property.

276. Moore, Emily. *Something to Count On*. New York:
     E.P. Dutton & Company, 1980. 103 pp. Ages 9-12.

     Ten-year-old Lorraine's parents are divorced and
     her father is always breaking his promises to
     come to see her and her little brother. Her be-
     havior problems at school are aggravated by her
     family situation and eased by an understanding
     new teacher.


277. Newfield, Marcia. *A Book for Jodan*. New York:
     Atheneum, 1975. Illustrations by Diane de Groat.
     48 pp. Ages 7-11.

     When Jodan learns that her parents are separating,
     she wonders if she is to blame and what can be
     done to keep them together. Emphasis is on the
     long-distance separation Jodan must deal with
     when she and her mother move to California and
     her father remains in Massachusetts. On one of
     her visits, Jodan's father gives her a wonderful
     present that makes her realize that she is still
     very important to him.


278. Noble, June. *Two Homes for Lynn*. New York:
     Holt, Rinehart & Winston, 1979. Illustrations
     by Yuri Salzman. 29 pp. Ages 6-8.

     Six-year-old Lynn's make-believe friend helps
     her adjust to her two homes after her parents'
     divorce.


279. Norris, Gunilla B. *Lillan*. New York: Atheneum,
     1968. Illustrated by Nancie Swanberg. 137 pp.

     This story, set in Sweden, centers around a pre-
     adolescent girl's fear of being unloved. Lillan's
     parents are divorced and her father has moved to
     another part of the world. Lillan is certain she
     will lose her mother who has begun dating.

280. Okimoto, Jean Davies. *My Mother Is Not Married to My Father*. New York: G.P. Putnam's Sons, 1979. 109 pp. Ages 9-12.

    Eleven-year-old Cynthia and her six-year-old sister try to adjust to their parents' separation and divorce. In addition, they have to cope with the fact that each parent is dating other people and the girls have to share their mother and father with others. One particularly sensitive incident concerns a school play attended by the parents, each with a new friend. Cynthia is quite confused about all those people, who are her family, yet no one is married.

281. Perl, Lila. *The Telltale Summer of Tina C*. New York: Seabury Press, 1975. 160 pp. Ages 10-13.

    Already unsure of herself, twelve-year-old Tina is thrown into deeper confusion when she learns that her recently divorced parents both intend to remarry.

282. Perry, Patricia, and Marietta Lynch. *Mommy and Daddy Are Divorced*. New York: Dial Press, 1978. 26 pp. Ages 4-7.

    Preschool-age brothers describe what they do with their father when he visits and what they do alone at home with their mother. Beautiful photographs.

283. Pevsner, Stella. *A Smart Kid Like You*. New York: Seabury Press, 1975. 216 pp. Ages 11-14.

    Just as Nina begins to accept her parents' divorce, she discovers her father's new wife is to be her seventh-grade math teacher. During her first

year in junior high, she begins to adjust to her
father's new home, the new school with old and
new friends, and her mother's dating.

284.  Pfeffer, Susan Beth. *Marly the Kid*. New York:
      Doubleday & Company, 1975. Ages 11-14.

      Marly runs away from her mother to live with her
      father and new stepmother. She settles in to
      tenth grade and adjusts to a new home and school,
      until she refuses to take insulting remarks from
      her history teacher. Her stepmother is a support-
      ive adult in this crisis.

285.  Robson, Bonnie. *My Parents Are Divorced Too:
      Teenagers Talk about Their Experiences and How
      They Cope*. New York: Everest House, 1980.
      208 pp. Young adults.

      Interviews with twenty-eight young people who
      explore their understanding of their parents'
      divorce, what caused it, their feelings about it,
      and how they coped with it. Book focuses on
      different issues such as how they were told,
      parents' dating, remarriage, and siblings. Quo-
      tations from the interviews are used, often in
      a disjointed manner. Psychiatrist-author ends
      each chapter with a list of short general sugges-
      tions for adolescents and for parents. Some adoles-
      cents might find this book helpful in articu-
      lating feelings.

286.  Rogers, Helen Spelman. *Morris and His Brave
      Lion*. New York: McGraw-Hill Book Company, 1975.
      Illustrated by Glo Coalson. 48 pp. Ages 4-8.

      Lonely for his father after his parents' di-
      vorce, a little boy thinks of a way of bringing
      his father back to see him.

287. Schuchman, Joan. *Two Places to Sleep*. Minneapolis: Carol Rhoda Books, 1979. Illustrated by Jim LaMarch. 28 pp. Ages 7-11.

David describes living with his father and visiting his mother on weekends after his parents' divorce. He discusses his feelings and his fears about the divorce and how it is affecting his life.

288. Sinberg, Janet. *Divorce is a Grown-Up Problem: A Book about Divorce for Young Children and Their Parents*. New York: Avon Books, 1978. Illustrated by Nancy Gray. 47 pp. Ages 4-6.

In this story written to help a child understand what has happened to a divorcing family, the author acknowledges that it is a confusing, angry, and painful time for the parents and the children. The book may encourage children to begin exploring and expressing their feelings. See also entry 295.

289. Slote, Alfred. *Love and Tennis*. New York: Macmillan Publishing Company, 1979. 163 pp. Ages 11-14.

A fifteen-year-old tennis player's experience in a world of competitive sports help him come to terms with his parents' divorce, his first romance, and his own ambition.

290. ———. *Matt Gargan's Boy*. New York: J.B. Lippincott Company, 1975. 159 pp. Ages 8-11.

A major leaguer's son feels threatened when a girl tries out for his little league baseball team and his divorced mother becomes interested in the girl's father.

291.  Sobol, Harriet Langsam. *My Other-Mother, My
      Other-Father*. New York: Macmillan Publishing
      Company, 1979. Photographs by Patricia Agre.
      34 pp. Ages 8-10.

      Twelve-year-old Andrea, whose parents have di-
      vorced and remarried, discusses the complexities
      of her new, larger family. In a simple, straight-
      forward manner, this book attempts to explore the
      feelings, tensions, and problems created in the
      lives of children whose family life has been dis-
      rupted in this manner. Teacher plays a helpful
      role.

292.  Spilke, Francine. *The Family that Changed*. New
      York: Crown Publishers, 1979. Illustrated by
      Tom O'Sullivan. 32 pp. Ages 4-6.

      Provides an explanation to preschoolers about
      why and how families change with divorce. Illus-
      trations are age-appropriate; text may be too
      wordy for preschoolers. Written to go with a
      manual for parents by the same author; see entry
      221.

293.  Stanek, Muriel. *I Won't Go Without a Father*.
      Chicago: Albert Whitman and Company, 1972.
      Illustrations by Eleanor Mill. 32 pp. Ages 5-8.

      Steve, whose father is not living with him,
      thinks he will be the only child at the school
      open house without a father. The author accomp-
      lishes two very important things with this story.
      She legitimizes an emotion that often makes chil-
      dren feel ashamed and allows those children to
      accept themselves. In addition, she exposes
      this particular situation to youngsters in two-
      parent families who may be unaware of various
      family structures.

294. Stein, Sara Bonnett. *On Divorce: An Open Family Book for Parents and Children Together.* New York: Walker Publishing Company, 1979. Photographs by Erika Stone. Ages 5-8.

Separate text for parents and children explores various emotions aroused by divorce in a friend's family. Vivid photographs. The scope makes it a perceptive book to share with children whose own families are intact.

295. Stenson, Janet Sinberg. *Now I Have a Stepparent and It's Kind of Confusing.* New York: Avon Books, 1979. Illustrated by Nancy Gray. 42 pp. Ages 4-6.

This book, a sequel to *Divorce is a Grown Up Problem* (entry 288), describes a child's confusing and scary feelings about the new relationship. Talking about feelings and receiving reassurances indicate model behavior for children and adults.

296. Stoltz, Mary. *Leap Before You Look.* New York: Harper & Row, 1972. 259 pp. Ages 12 and up.

Fourteen-year-old Janine is stunned and enraged when divorce forces her, her mother, and younger brother to move into her grandmother's house. Over the course of the next year, she takes a closer look at other people's families in the hope of making some sense of her own. The realization that other people have problems, too, and that life goes on allows her gradually to adjust to her father's remarriage.

297. Thomas, Ianthe. *Eliza's Daddy.* New York: Harcourt Brace Jovanovich, 1976. Illustrated by Moneta Barnett. 64 pp. Ages 4-8.

Eliza's parents are divorced and she lives with
her mother. Her father comes to visit Eliza
every Saturday. More than anything, she wants
to visit her father's new family--she is especially interested in his stepdaughter who is the
same age as she.

298.   The Unit at Fayerweather Street School. *The Kid's
       Book of Divorce: By, For and About Kids.* Lexing-
       ton, Mass.: Lewis Publishing Company, 1981.
       123 pp. Ages 9-15.

       Twenty children, ages eleven to fourteen, discuss
       various aspects of divorce, including custody ar-
       rangements, parents' boyfriends and girlfriends,
       how they were first told about their parents' di-
       vorce, and how divorce has changed them. Addi-
       tional chapters reflect the children's feelings
       regarding the legal issues, getting help from
       counseling, and day-to-day living through the
       divorce. One particularly significant chapter
       entitled "Separation: It's Not the End of the
       World" honestly discusses the fears and pain
       that accompany the initial separation. Readers
       are assured that their emotions are normal and
       quite valid.

299.   Vigna, Judith. *She's Not My Real Mother.* Chi-
       cago: Albert Whitman & Company, 1980. 30 pp.
       Ages 4-6.

       Miles doesn't want to be friends with her. She's
       not his real mother. When he gets lost, however,
       his stepmother comes to his rescue, and he thinks
       maybe she could be a friend, not a mother.

300.   White, Ann S. *Divorce.* New York: Franklin Watts,
       1979. 55 pp. Ages 9-12.

Discusses the causes and procedures of divorce, the changes it brings to family life, and its effect on children.

301. Zolotow, Charlotte. *A Father Like That*. New York: Harper & Row, 1971. Illustrated by Ben Shecter. Ages 4-7.

A boy discusses with his mother the kind of father he imagines his unknown father could be. His mother responds that even if he never gets to know his father, he can be a father like that.

AUDIO-VISUAL RESOURCES

The films listed below are given as an additional resource for readers of this book.

Films and filmstrips can be used to initiate dis-
cussions in parents' or children's groups (e.g.,
*Divorce*, Parts I & II) or as an overview of the field
(e.g., *Children of Divorce*, NBC).
For a comprehensive article on using media on children and divorce, the author refers the reader to the
excellent filmography and accompanying article by Dr.
Edward Mason, listed in entry 115.


*Breakup.* 15 minutes, color, 1973. Producer: KETC-TV.
    Distributor: Agency for Instructional Television,
    Box A, Bloomington, IN  47401.


*Children of Divorce.* 37 minutes, color, 1976. Pro-
    ducer: NBC-TV. Distributor: Films Inc., 1144
    Wilmette Avenue, Wilmette, IL  60091.
    Barbara Walters, host.


*Children of Divorce--Transitional Issues for Elementary
    School;*
*Children of Divorce--Transitional Issues for Junior High
    and High School Ages.*
    American Personnel and Guidance Association Film

*111*

Department, 1607 New Hampshire Avenue N.W.,
Washington, DC 20009.
Set of films and vignettes.


*Divorce: For Better or for Worse.* 49 minutes, color,
1977. Producer: ABC-TV. Distributor: McGraw-
Hill Films, 1221 Avenue of the Americas, New York,
NY 10020.


*Divorce, Parts I & II.* 40 minutes, color, 1975.
Directors: Sheila Kessler and John M. Whitely.
Distributor: American Personnel and Guidance
Association, Film Department, 1607 New Hampshire
Avenue N.W., Washington, DC 20009.


*Family Matters.* 15 minutes, color, 1975. Producer:
Northern Virginia Educational Telecommunications
Association. Distributor: Agency for Instruction-
al Television, Box A, Bloomington, IN 47401.
Study guide available.


*The Greenbergs of California.* 59 minutes, color, 1977.
Director: Mark Obenhaus. Distributor: Carousel
Films, 1501 Broadway, New York, NY 10036.
From the Group W series *Six American Families.*


*Happily Unmarried.* 23 minutes, color, 1977. Director:
Lorna Rasmussen. Distributor: National Film
Board of Canada, 1251 Avenue of the Americas,
New York, NY 10020.


*Me and Dad's New Wife.* 33 minutes, color, 1976. Producer: Daniel Wilson. Starring Kristy McNichol.
Based on *A Smart Kid Like You* by Stella Pevsner.
Distributor: Time-Life Video Distribution Center,
100 Eisenhower, Paramus, NJ 07652.

*Mister Rogers Talks with Parents about Divorce.*
1 hour, 1981. Family Communications Inc., 4802
Fifth Avenue, Pittsburgh, PA 15213. Host Fred
Rogers, with guest Earl Grollman and a studio
audience of parents. Video-tape and transcript.


*Mothers After Divorce.* 20 minutes, color, 1976. Directors: Henry and Marilyn Felt. Distributor:
Polymorph Films, Boston, MA 02115.


*My Parents Are Getting a Divorce.* 20 minutes, 1980.
Human Relations Media. 175 Thompkins Avenue,
Pleasantville, NY 10570. Film strips and tape.
Part I, Separation; Part II, Adjusting.


*Not Together Now: End of a Marriage.* 25 minutes,
color, 1975. Director: Miriam Weinstein. Distributor: Polymorph Films, Boston, MA 02115.


*Raising Michael Alone.* 17 Minutes, color, 1976. Director: Henry Felt. Distributor: Education Development Center, 55 Chapel Street, Newton, MA
02160. Teacher's guide available.


*Separation/Divorce: It Has Nothing to Do with You.*
14 minutes, color, 1974. Producer: Steven Katten.
Distributor: CRM/McGraw-Hill Films, 110 15 Street,
Del Mar, CA 92014. Study guide available.


*Single Parent.* 42 minutes, color, 1976. Producer:
Hubert Smith. Distributor: The Media Guild,
P.O. Box 881, Solana Beach, CA 92075. Study
guide available.


*The Sky is Falling.* Filmstrip and Tape, 15 minutes,
color, 1978. Available from Dr. Margaret

Galante, Psychological Services, Union Free
School District, 99 Campus Drive, Port Washington, NY   11050.


*Stepparenting:  New Families, Old Ties*.   25 minutes,
color, 1976.   Directors: Henry and Marilyn Felt.
Distributor: Polymorph Films, Boston, MA   02115.

ORGANIZATIONAL RESOURCES

The organizations listed in this section offer information about programs, newsletters, and support services
for families experiencing divorce. National organizations such as Parents Without Partners have local chapters that provide local education and social programs
for parents and children. Other organizations are
clearinghouses for information (such as The Step
Family Foundation) or could help find a therapist (Family Service Association of America). Other organizations, such as The Divorce Resource and Mediation Center in Cambridge, Mass., provide services regionally.
These are listed here as a model of what to look for
in other areas.

To find local services, parents should consult
agencies serving families such as community health
centers, family service or youth service of the local
city or county, or child guidance centers. Clergy or
family counselors can refer parents locally for specific
services related to marriage, divorce, single parenting,
or remarriage. A listing of sources is included in the
yellow pages of telephone directories under lawyers,
marriage and family counseling, psychologists, and psy-
chotherapists.


*Alanon Family Group Headquarters*, 1 Park Avenue, New
York, NY 10016.

For help to families of alcoholics.


*American Association of Marriage and Family Therapists*,
924 West 9th Street, Upland, CA   91786.

For help in finding a therapist.


*American Psychiatric Association*, 1700 18th Street,
N.W., Washington, DC   20009.

For help in finding a therapist.


*American Psychological Association*, 1200 17th Street,
N.W., Washington, DC   20036.

For help in finding a therapist.


*American Society for Adolescent Psychiatry*, 24 Green
Valley Road, Wallingford, PA   19086.

For help in finding a therapist.


*Big Brothers/Big Sisters of America*, 117 South 17th
Street, Suite 1200, Philadelphia, PA   19103.


*Center for Families in Transition*, 5725 Paradise Drive,
Corte Madeira, CA   94925.

Center pursuing next five years of Wallerstein
and Kelly study.


*Center for Legal Psychiatry*, 2424 Wilshire Boulevard,
Santa Monica, CA   90403.

For divorce and custody counseling.

*Center for Parenting Studies*, Wheelock College, 200
    The Riverway, Boston, MA   02215.

    For publications and seminars on parenting for
    professionals and parents: *Children of Divorce*,
    *Parenting after Divorce*, *Work and Families*.


*Custody Action for Lesbian Mothers*, P.O. Box 281,
    Narberth, PA   19072.


*Displaced Homemakers Network*, 755 8th Street N.W.,
    Washington, DC   20001.

    For information about reentry into job market.


*Divorce Resource and Mediation Center, Inc.*, 2464
    Massachusetts Avenue, Cambridge, MA   02140.

    Provides services for individuals, couples, and
    families in the area of support groups, indivi-
    dual and group therapy, mediation, and marriage
    and remarriage counseling.  Serves the New Eng-
    land region, but similar services are available
    in other states.  See entries 96 and 97.


*The Family Center*, 210 California Avenue, Suite 6,
    Palo Alto, CA   94306.

    Parent groups and mediation counseling.  See
    entry 126.


*Family Mediation Association*, 2380 S.W. 34th Way,
    Fort Lauderdale, FL   33310.

    For names of trained mediators.

*Family Resource/Referral Center National Council on Family Relations*, 1219 University Avenue S.E., Minneapolis, MN 55414.

*Family Service Association of America*, 44 East 23rd Street, New York, NY 10010.

> For guidance in finding the right kind of assistance in local areas.

*MOMMA*, P.O. Box 5759, Santa Monica, CA 90405.

> Organization for single mothers; has local chapters. See entry 202.

*National Association of Social Workers*, 1425 H Street, N.W., Suite 600, Washington, DC 20005.

> For help in finding a therapist.

*National Committee for Citizens in Education*, Suite 410, Wilde Lake Village Green, Dept. SP, Columbia, MD 21044.

> For mobilizing schools to respond to needs of single parents. See entry 41.

*National Institute for Professional Training in Divorce Counseling*, 1295 Lenox Circle, N.E., Atlanta, GA 30306.

> Information about divorce adjustment groups in local area.

*National Single Parent Coalition*, 10 West 23rd Street, New York, NY 10010.

*North American Conference of Separated and Divorced
Catholics*, The Paulist Center, 5 Park Street,
Boston, MA   02108.


*Parents Without Partners*, 7910 Woodmont Avenue, Suite
1000, Washington, DC   20014.

> For information and programs about single parent-
> hood; local chapters in U.S. and Canada. Has a
> newsletter, *The Single Parent* ($2.75/year for
> members, $5.50/year for nonmembers).


*Remarried Incorporated*, Box 742, Santa Ana, CA   92701.

> For information about programs for stepfamilies
> that may be social, educational, or cultural in
> nature.


*Single Dad's Life Style*, Box 4842, Scottsdale, AZ
85258.

> In addition to the monthly journal ($1/single
> copy; $12/year), Bob Hirschfeld publishes an
> annual list in the February issue of fathers'
> rights groups, by state.


*Stepfamily Association of America*, Palo Alto, CA.

> See entry 159.


*The Step Family Foundation*, 333 West End Avenue,
New York, NY   10023.

> Clearinghouse of information and research on
> stepfamilies.  See entry 218.

*Stepparent's Forum*, Westmount, P.O. Box 4002, Montreal,
    H3I 2X3, Canada.

    Periodical designed to offer support and guidance
    to stepparents.

# INDEX

Abarbanel, Alice, 1
Abt, Lawrence E., 152
Adams, Florence, 235
Adams, Gerald R., 60
Adams, Paul L., 147
Adler, C.S., 236
Adolescents, 7, 28, 70, 99, 111, 121, 125, 127, 128,
        132, 136, 149, 162, 165, 169, 175, 181, 204
Ages: see Preschoolers, Elementary school-age children,
        Adolescents
Ahrons, Constance, 2
Alexander, Ann, 237
Alexander, Sharon, 3,4
Allers, Robert, 5
Anderson, Hilary, 6
Andrew, Jan, 238
Atkin, Edith, 7, 22

Baden, Clifford, 8, 9
Baird, Kay L., 148
Ballantine, Constance, 75
Beal, Edward W., 10
Benedek, Elissa P., 11, 12, 13, 14, 44, 246
Benedek, Richard S., 11, 12, 13, 14, 44
Berg, Berthold, 15
Berg-Cross, Gary, 128
Berg-Cross, Linda, 128
Berger, Terry, 239
Berman, Claire, 183

Turow, Rita, 224
Tynan, Susan A., 157

Victor, Ira, 158
Vigna, Judith, 299
Viscott, David, 264
Visher, Emily B., 159, 160
Visher, John S., 159, 160
Visiting, 3, 9, 14, 95, 127, 130, 131, 135, 144, 154,
    168, 177, 189, 206, 220, 225

Walker, Libby, 161
Wallerstein, Judith S., 8, 44, 94, 95, 129, 162–169,
    185, 186, 198, 226, 227
Warner, Nancy S., 80
Warshak, Richard, 140
Weber, Ruth E., 66
Wechsler, Ralph C., 75
Weingarten, Helen, 101
Weinglass, Janet, 170
Weinstein, Jeffrey, 61
Weisfeld, David, 171
Weiss, Robert S., 8, 172, 173, 174, 175, 176
Wheeler, Michael, 177
White, Ann S., 300
Wilkie, Jane, 299
Wilkinson, Gary S., 179
Willis, Irene, 127
Willison, Marilyn Murray, 230
Winkler, Win Ann, 158
Woody, J.D., 180
Woolley, Persia, 232, 233

Young, David, 181
Young, Hope, 202
Young, James J., 182
Young, Karol, 202
Young, Nancy, 202

Zill, Nicholas, 8
Zolotow, Charlotte, 301